New Mermaids

BEN JONSON

The Alchemist

Edited by Elizabeth Cook

A & C BLACK • LONDON
W W NORTON • NEW YORK

Second edition 1991
Reprinted 1992, 1993, 1995, 1997, 1998, 2001, 2004, 2006
A & C Black Publishers Limited
38 Soho Square, London, W1D 3HB
www.acblack.com

ISBN–10: 0–7136–7104–1
ISBN–13: 978–0–7136–7104–9

First New Mermaid edition 1966 by Ernest Benn Limited
(edited by Douglas Brown and, following his death in 1964,
completed by Brian Morris and Philip Brockbank)
© 1996 Ernest Benn Limited

Published in the United States of America by
W.W. Norton & Company Inc.
500 Fifth Avenue, New York, N.Y. 10110

ISBN 0–393–90056–8

A CIP catalogue record for this book
is available from the British Library.

This book is produced using paper that is made from wood grown in
managed, sustainable forests. It is natural, renewable and recyclable.
The logging and manufacturing processes conform to the environmental
regulations of the country of origin.

Printed in Great Britain by
Bookmarque Ltd, Croydon, Surrey

CONTENTS

ACKNOWLEDGEMENTS

I have drawn gratefully on the work of many previous editors of Jonson's works and of *The Alchemist* in particular. Of the greatest resource have been the following works which I list chronologically:

John Upton, *Remarks on Three Plays of Benjamin Jonson, viz Volpone, Epicoene, and The Alchimist*, London, 1749
The Works of Ben Jonson, ed. William Gifford, 3 vols., London, 1816
The Alchemist, ed. C. M. Hathaway, New Haven, 1903
Ben Jonson, ed. C. H. Herford, P. & E. Simpson, 11 vols., Oxford, 1925–52
The Alchemist, ed. D. Brown, London, 1966
The Alchemist, ed. F. H. Mares, London, 1967
The Alchemist, ed. A. Kernan, New Haven, 1974
Ben Jonson, ed. Ian Donaldson, Oxford, 1985

INTRODUCTION

The Author

Ben Jonson was born a Londoner in 1572, the posthumous son of an impoverished gentleman. His mother married a bricklayer shortly afterwards, and his circumstances in youth were decidedly straitened. Through the intervention of an outsider, however, he had some education at Westminster School under William Camden, who remained a lifelong friend; but he probably did not finish school and certainly did not go on, as most of his contemporaries there did, to Oxford or Cambridge. Instead he was apprenticed, probably in his stepfather's craft, about 1589, remaining in it long enough only to learn he 'could not endure' it. Before 1597 he had volunteered to serve in Flanders where, during a lull in the fighting, 'in the face of both the camps', he met and killed one of the enemy in single combat and returned from no-man's-land with his victim's weapons. The scene is an emblem for his life: the giant figure, a party to neither faction, warring alone in the classical manner before his awed onlookers.

Sometime in the early 1590s he married. By the time he was twenty-five he was playing the lead in Kyd's *Spanish Tragedy* for the theatrical manager and entrepreneur Philip Henslowe. As a writer he may also have composed additions to Kyd's work; he certainly did so for Nashe's satirical *Isle of Dogs*, and was imprisoned for the 'slandrous matter' in it. But already by 1598 Francis Meres listed him in *Palladis Tamia* amongst 'our best for tragedy' along with Kyd himself and Shakespeare. These tragedies, and indeed all the work of his early twenties, have vanished, but in the surviving records the man bursts upon the theatrical scene with characteristic and transforming energy.

In 1598 as well his first great success in comedy, *Every Man in his Humour*, was produced; in this, as in *Sejanus*, Shakespeare played a leading role. Within the same month Jonson killed an actor in Henslowe's company, Gabriel Spencer, in a duel. He pleaded guilty to a charge of felony and saved himself from the gallows only by claiming 'benefit of clergy', that is, by proving his literacy and hence immunity by reading 'neck-verse'. His goods – such as they may have been – were confiscated and he was branded on the thumb. His career was not yet fully under way: in writing of the incident, Henslowe refers to Jonson as a 'bricklayer'.

Still in the same year *The Case is Altered* was acted, once again with great success, and in 1599 or 1600 came *Every Man Out of his Humour*, which – although it too enhanced his growing reputation – included in the targets of its satire the diction of some contemporary playwrights, notably John Marston. Marston may have annoyed his older friend by a bungled attempt to flatter him in *Histriomastix* a few months earlier, but he was in any case ready to take very unfriendly revenge for *Every Man Out* when, in late 1600, he caricatured Jonson in *Jack Drum's Entertainment.* Jonson countered with *Cynthia's Revels*, Marston with *What You Will*, Jonson with *Poetaster*, all in 1601. Thomas Dekker, previously Jonson's collaborator on the lost tragedy *Page of Plymouth*, came to Marston's aid with *Satiro-mastix*. But Jonson had gone beyond attacking his attackers: his plays, and particularly *Poetaster*, satirized influential men, and he barely escaped prosecution again. He withdrew, not yet thirty years old, from comedy and the popular stage, into the patronage and protection first of Sir Robert Townshend and later Esmé Stewart, Lord Aubigny, to whom he dedicated the fruit of his retirement, *Sejanus.*

Once again Jonson's talent for trouble caused him difficulty with the authorities, this time on the pretext of 'popery and treason' – he had become a Catholic during his imprisonment for killing Spencer – and once again powerful friends intervened to save him. Still again in 1604, when he collaborated with his reconciled friend Marston and with George Chapman on the comedy *Eastward Ho!* he was jailed, now for satirizing the Scots, for James I was king. But once more he was let off, and on the whole the accession of James I was of great benefit to Jonson: for this brilliant and learned court he wrote almost all his many masques, delicate confections of erudition and artistry in which he knew no master.

But it is to *Volpone* (1605), *Epicoene* (1609–10), *The Alchemist* (1610), *Bartholmew Fair* (1614) and *The Devil is an Ass* (1616) that we must turn for the central documents of his comic maturity, interrupted only by the tragic (and unsuccessful) *Catiline* of 1611. Jonson had by 1612 become conscious of the scope of his accomplishment, for in that year he began work on a collective edition which would enshrine in an impressive folio the authoritative text. His close connections with the court, doubtless enhanced when he gave up Catholicism about 1610, and the literary self-awareness begot by his huge reading in the classics, in part recorded in his common-place book *Timber*, led him, unique amongst the playwrights of his age, to take such pains with his *oeuvre.*

Jonson continued writing his masques and non-dramatic poems, but no stage play appeared after *The Devil is an Ass* until *The Staple of News* in 1625. Jonson's fortune declined in the nine years between. He began them with a walking tour of Scotland in 1618, where Drummond recorded their *Conversations*, and with a visit to Oxford in 1619, where the University made him a Master of Arts. He ended them increasingly destitute of health, money and invention. His rule over the 'tribe' that met at the Mermaid was unweakened, but he depended more and more on pensions from Crown and City, especially when he failed to maintain with Charles I the favour he had found with the scholarly James I.

There followed *The New Inn* (1629), *The Magnetic Lady* (1632), and *The Tale of a Tub* (1633); the first was a disaster the last two did little to mitigate. Apart from a few verses he wrote nothing thereafter (his *English Grammar*, a draft of which perished in the fire that destroyed his library in 1623, probably goes back to a period as Professor of Rhetoric at Gresham College), although his lifelong habit of reading was not broken. He did not complete work on the second folio which was to include his writings since 1612. No child of his survived him, and it fell to his intellectual disciples, the 'Sons of Ben', to be his literary executors.

He died on 6 August 1637, at the age of sixty-five, and was buried in Westminster Abbey.

DATE AND SOURCES

The Alchemist was entered into the Stationers' Register on 3 October 1610. The earliest performance of which a record has been found was in Oxford in September 1610.[1] The King's Men, unable to play in London where the theatres had been closed since July on account of the plague, had gone on tour with *The Alchemist* and *Othello*. Some think it unlikely that Jonson would have premiered new work outside London and suggest that the play's first performance must have taken place earlier in 1610, before the company's exile in July. Without new evidence it is impossible to be sure but, since the play's whole fiction revolves around the situation of waiting for the plague to abate and taking advantage of the intervening time, it seems possible that the King's Men were doing perforce what many of today's companies choose to do – previewing their work in the provinces before a London run. Mammon promises 'to fright the plague/Out o' the kingdom, in three months'; Surly comments, 'And I'll/Be bound the players shall sing your praises, then,/Without their poets' (II.i.69–72). Perhaps poet Jonson scripted this in reference to his own players' impatience to get back within the city liberties.

If that were the case it would be in keeping with a play highly specific about the time and place of its setting, both of which nearly coincide with the circumstances of its early performances. The year is 1610 (the

---

[1] See Geoffrey Tillotson, '*Othello* and *The Alchemist* at Oxford in 1610', in *The Times Literary Supplement*, 20 July 1933, p. 494.

nineteen-year-old widow was born in 1591 [II.vi.31; IV.iv.29–30] and Ananias confirms this date [V.v.105]). The date of the play's fictional setting is either 23 October or 1 November.[1]

The F text of the play lists the 'principall Comœdians' – the actors from the King's Men – who took part in the play's first performance. They are well-known names: Richard Burbage, John Lowin, John Hemminges, Henry Condel, William Ostler, William Eglestone, Robert Armin, Nicholas Tooley, Alexander Cooke, John Underwood. The King's Men had begun to use the theatre at Blackfriars as their winter house as an alternative to the Globe in 1609.[2] There is no external evidence as to which London theatre *The Alchemist* first played in but, given the play's fictional setting in Blackfriars (where Jonson also lived), it is very probable that Jonson anticipated using that theatre. He seems to have intended a great measure of coincidence between the circumstances of his fiction and those of an actual production in the date and location of his play.

There is no single source to the play though, as Alvin Kernan has pointed out, the plot is of a familiar farce type which involves the attempt to keep various individuals apart at all costs.[3] There is a loose parallel between the situation of *The Alchemist* and that of Plautus' *Mostellaria* in which a servant abuses his absent master's trust in a comparable way. Jonson would have known this as he would have known other literary treatments of bogus, profiteering alchemists, such as Erasmus' colloquy *De Alcumista* and Chaucer's *Canon's Yeoman's Tale*. But these works can in no sense be called 'sources.'

The play is, however, deeply informed by Jonson's extensive reading. '*Language* most shewes a man: speake that I may see thee'.[4] Jonson's belief that a man, as it were, speaks himself, to some extent relieved him of the burden of pastiche and he allows the occult and puritan writers from whose works he incorporates whole chunks to damn themselves with their own words. Dol, in her 'fit', recites passages from Hugh Broughton's *A Concent of Scripture*. Subtle's explanation of the alchemical process in II.iii. is

---

[1] Ananias provides two possible dates in terms of his non-conformist calendar which makes March the first month (since, according to Puritans, this was the month of the Creation). In III.ii.131–2 Ananias estimates that in fifteen days time it will be 'the second day, of the third week,/In the ninth month'– i.e. 16 November, which gives 1 November as the date of the play's fiction. However, in V.v. 101–5 Ananias gives the date on which the Brethren's pounds were 'told out' as 'the second day of the fourth week,/In the eighth month . . . The year, of the last patience of the Saints,/Six hundred and ten.' This translates as 23 October; but perhaps Ananias is referring to an event before the start of the play.

[2] E. K. Chambers, *The Elizabethan Stage*, 4 vols., Oxford, 1951 (repr.) vol. ii, pp. 509–10.

[3] *The Alchemist*, ed. Alvin Kernan, New Haven, 1974, p. 243.

[4] *H.&S.*, vol. viii, p. 625.

taken – at times verbatim – from Martin Delrio's *Disquisitiones Magicae*. In *Volpone* the gentleman-traveller, Peregrine, agrees with Sir Politic that the mountebank's language is 'rare': 'But alchemy,/I never heard the like – or Broughton's books' (II.ii.118–19). In *The Alchemist* Jonson does not tamper with the rare languages of Broughton and alchemy – except to lift them out of any context where it is possible to take them seriously. *H.&S.* also record quotations from Arnold of Villa Nova's *Rosarium Philosophorum* (II.i.39,40; II.iii. 106–14), Geber's *Summa Perfectionis* (II.v.35–6), Paracelsus' *Manuale de Lapide Philosophico* (II.ii.25–8, II.v.28), and Robertus Vallensis' *De Veritate et Antiquitate Artis Chemicae* (II.i.101–4).

Jonson, whose plays are so full of the circumstantial reality of Jacobean life, incorporates current news into the play. Fifty years later Margaret of Newcastle was to develop the hypothesis that Jonson's satire was specifically directed at the Elizabethan occultist, John Dee, and his assistant, Edward Kelley, Dol and Dame Pliant representing their two, pooled, wives.[1] The play's satire is clearly wider than this suggestion allows but John Dee does appear in Abel Drugger's rebus and Jonson's knowledge of him and Kelley is part of the play's context. The gulling of the credulous Dapper by the Queen of Fairy had a contemporary parallel in the case of Thomas Rogers, a Dorset man of marriageable age, who was robbed of £6 by two brothers who promised him an introduction to the Fairy Queen who would then willingly be his bride. This case came to Chancery between November 1609 and February 1610.[2] The hint Jonson takes from this news item reflects his alertness to any material which could be of use.

ALCHEMY AND WIT

The Alchemist is often described as if it were a satire which exposed the fraudulence of alchemy – the process which transforms base metals into gold. In fact Jonson's play is neither exposure nor celebration of alchemy *per se*: Subtle and Face, the two central characters, though sufficiently learned in alchemical lore to awe their clients, are not alchemists but con men.

A true alchemist would, almost of necessity, be hard to identify. Successful alchemical projection was believed to require not only an absolutely meticulous attention to material requirements but also a rare spiritual purity of the practitioner. One might go so far as to say that the Philosopher's Stone, so avidly sought by the greedy, would only be granted to a person so free of self interest as not to want it. A person of such purity – without

[1] ibid., vol. x, p. 47.
[2] ibid., vol. x, pp. 47–8.

cupidity or material ambition – would hardly care to try whether they could indeed make material gold. Their goal would be an alchemy and regeneration of the spirit beside which the power to transmute metals would appear a negligible trick and not one to be advertised.[1]

Inevitably it was the charlatans and profiteers who were most in evidence, not those on the path to true alchemy. Nevertheless there were some who, while not successful, were not knowing frauds. They might themselves have attributed their failure to their lack of spiritual development, or to some error in the minutely demanding material process. Such may have been Cornelius de Lannoy whom Elizabeth I imprisoned when he failed to come up with the stone. He pleaded that 'if it shall please the Queen to release him from confinement he will without delay put into operation that wonderful elixir for making gold for her majesty's service'.[2]

Subtle speaks of being 'locked up, in the Tower, forever,/ To make gold there (for th' state)' (IV.vii.81–2) and, though Elizabeth's patronage of learned occultists such as John Dee was not primarily from mercenary motives, alchemy was clearly seen as a means of replenishing state coffers. But such hopes misunderstood the nature of the Philosopher's Stone whose virtue (meaning both 'power' and 'goodness' and 'power through goodness') could never become a transferable commodity.

The virtue (power to do good) of the stone is both consequence and symbol of the virtue (powerful because good) of its possessor. Sir Epicure Mammon, the play's master consumer, does not grasp this. He believes that the stone is able to originate the virtue which it reflects and answers in its possessor. He believes that the stone 'by its virtue,/Can confer honour, love, respect, long life,/Give safety, valour: yea, and victory,/To whom he will' (II.i.49–52). Later Subtle cautions him that the man who will possess the stone must be *'homo frugi,/*A pious, holy, and religious man,/One free from mortal sin, a very virgin.' That, as Mammon sees it, is Subtle the 'alchemist's' business – 'That makes it, sir, he is so.' For himself he promises a shorter way, 'But I buy it' (II.ii.97–100).

This more everyday alchemy – by which money is converted into commodity and stuff converted into revenue – is in evidence throughout the play. The first mention of the Philosopher's Stone is as a synonym for a source of profit:

[1] For more information on this more reputable alchemical tradition see Frances A. Yates, *The Rosicrucian Enlightenment,* London, 1972 (particularly chapter 14) and Allen G. Debus, *The English Paracelsians,* London, 1965.

[2] Quoted by Hathaway in the introduction to his edition of *The Alchemist,* New York, 1903, p. 37.

> I will have
> A book, but barely reckoning thy impostures,
> Shall prove a true philosopher's stone, to printers.   (I.i.101–2)

Alchemy also comes up in this first scene as a metaphor for social transformation. Subtle reminds Face of how he 'Sublimed [him], and exalted [him], and fixed [him]/I' the third region' (I.i.68–9). Subtle has 'translated' Face, and in turn the two of them find in the base matter of their fellow citizens a propensity to be converted into profit. When Face confronts Subtle with the claim that his contribution is indispensible, the 'stuff' he refers to is human stuff:

> You must have stuff, brought home to you, to work on?
> And, yet, you think, I am at no expense,
> In searching out these veins, then following 'em,
> Then trying 'em out.   (I.iii. 104–7)

These words are echoed by Mammon in the next act. But this time they refer to lead and iron:

> My only care is,
> Where to get stuff, enough now, to project on,
> This town will not half serve me.   (II.ii.11–13)

The pretence of alchemy at the centre of the play's plot acts most powerfully as a metaphor and an example of the several kinds of transformation – social, linguistic and economic – which concern the play's personnel. The charade of alchemy acts as a kind of cartoon or emblem of this more generally diffused process.

But while Face and Subtle's highly informed pretence of alchemy is the play's central unifying metaphor, it is only one of their several means of transforming unpromising stuff into the means of personal gain. The city which Jonson portrays is populated by citizens on the make. The play reflects a period and an environment of rapid upward mobility in which landed wealth began to be superseded by wealth from other sources and the kind of 'modern happiness' by which a Dol Common could become a great lady was more available than before. This kind of social alchemy can be seen in such details as the kinds of utensils possessed by working people. In 1577 William Harrison recorded that, in his part of Essex, villagers had replaced their 'treen' (wooden) platters with pewter, and that instead of wooden spoons they now used implements made of silver or tin.[1] Such transformations were considerably more rapid in the city.

All the inhabitants of the play share a hunger for upward mobility: they want not just wealth, but its accoutrements. Face describes Subtle's wonderful powers in terms of the kind of credit his clients might reasonably come to expect:

> You shall have a cast commander, (can but get
> In credit with a glover, or a spurrier,
> For some two pair, of either's ware, aforehand)
> Will, by most swift posts, dealing with him,
> Arrive at competent means, to keep himself,
> His punk, and naked body, in excellent fashion.
> And be admired for it.   (III.iv.76–82)

A credit limit which once extended only to the cost of two pairs of gloves will now stretch to stylish clothes for an entire household. But, significantly, this household does not comprise a nuclear family; the other occupants – the kept woman and the catamite – are also status commodities. This is the world which Jonson vilifies in his 'Epistle to a Friend to persuade him to the Wars' – a world in which bonds of affection have been replaced by acquisition and purchase and 'Adulteries . . . [are] grown commodities upon exchange.' In *The Alchemist* we see the nubile widow, Dame Pliant, being used as a transferable promissory note, offered in several extremities though only 'cashed in' by Lovewit at the end.

But though he recognised and castigated the moral depletion of the 'money get' age in which all is reduced to commodity, Jonson was clearly intrigued by the curious equivalences between stuffs that market valuations could create. The so-called 'commodity swindle' is mentioned twice in the play. This was the practice by which a money-lender would take advantage of his client in order to force him to accept part of the loan in unwanted commodities which he wished to offload – 'be it pepper, soap,/Hops, or tobacco, oatmeal, woad, or cheeses' (III.iv.97–8) – at inflated valuations.

The gulls – consumers to a man – reveal their imaginative scope in terms of their material ambitions, and it is revealing of the Puritans' pinched minds that what they want out of Subtle is, specifically, coin. All the others expect their investment to lead to some kind of transformation, but the Puritans just want more of the same. The only scope available to them

[1] William Harrison, *Description of England* (1577), ed. G. Edelen, New York, 1968, pp. 200–1.

is the minute room for play within the quibble between 'coining' and 'casting' (III.ii.151–2).

Face likes coins as well as wealth. With their various heads they are emblems of himself. At the end of Act III scene iv he empties Dapper's purse in the name of obtaining gratuities for the Fairy Queen's retinue. Dapper hands over 'six score Edward shillings . . . an old Harry's sovereign . . . three James shillings, and an Elizabeth groat . . ., Just twenty nobles'. Face urges more, 'I would you had the other noble in Marys.' Dapper has 'some Philip, and Marys'. 'Ay, those same/Are best of all', says Face. He is not simply greedy: he is an amateur numismatist taking pleasure in the individual particulars of coins and not just in their equivalent value. In this he recalls a character in a play written by Dekker ten years before *The Alchemist*. Firk, in *The Shoemaker's Holiday*, is given a threepenny bit which, for a moment, he thinks only three ha'pence till the contours of the coin impress him: 'yes, tis three pence, I smell the rose' (III.ii. 120–1). Such attention to the particulars of coins is absent from the majority of 'city comedies' whose concern is predominantly the way in which all relations are subjected to the law of commodity exchange. In these plays – such as Middleton's *A Mad World my Masters* (published in 1608) – coin, rather than coins, exists as a token of exchange. Correspondingly, the language of other city comedies lacks the textural variation to be found in *The Alchemist,* for words too are used more as equivalents, coins for exchange rather than collection. Thomas Hobbes was to express a view of words as tokens of exchange, of no intrinsic value: 'words are wise mens counters, they do but reckon by them: but they are the mony of fooles'.[1]

Pecuniary metaphors for language are so common as to be dead. We speak of word 'coining' and linguistic 'currency'. Word coining, and the exhilaration of it, are much in evidence in *The Alchemist*. Dapper is as eager to acquire and display a new word as the watch of which he claims to have been robbed. 'What do you think of me', he asks Face who has urged discretion, 'That I am a *Chiause*?' 'What's that?' asks Face, with the rest of us. 'The Turk was, here – /As one would say, do you think I am a Turk?' (I.ii.25–7). Kastril, called upon to quarrel with Surly, is moderately inventive. He calls Surly 'a shad, a whit,/A very tim' (IV.vii.45–6). Were this one-sided *flyting* match to develop we would expect more dictionary-eluding words.

The world of this play is cognate with that of the 'coney-catching' pamphlets of Dekker and Greene which provided the respectable (and expanding) reading public with titillating access to thieves' (coney-catchers')

---

[1] Thomas Hobbes, *Leviathan* (1651), ed. C. B. Macpherson, Harmondsworth, 1968, p. 106.

practices, including their 'cant' or jargon.[1] Surly, himself a card-sharp, knows this world and its language well enough; he sustains the coney-catching metaphor throughout his commentary in II.iii. As far as he is concerned the alchemical jargon used by Subtle and Face is another exclusive language of the same sort: 'What a brave language here is? Next to canting?' (II.iii.42).

Word-lover Dapper 'Consorts with the small poets of the time' and can 'court/His mistress out of Ovid' (I.ii.52, 57–58). Sir Epicure Mammon's love of eloquence is on a grander scale. He imagines himself able to purchase the word-power of others:

> my flatterers
> Shall be the pure, and gravest of Divines,
> That I can get for money. My mere fools,
> Eloquent burgesses, and then my poets,
> The same that writ so subtly of the fart,
> Whom I will entertain, still, for that subject.'   (II.ii.59–64)

For Mammon the worth of words lies in the glamour of their surface effects, not in their meaning. Webster's Duchess of Malfi does not lose sight of the fact of death when she contemplates its various forms:

> What would it pleasure me to have my throat cut
> With diamonds? or to be smothered
> With cassia? or to be shot to death with pearls?   (IV.ii.216–18)

But one can imagine Mammon relishing the prospect of deaths so expensive, as if the instruments could confer luxury. His use of words is sensual and associative – poetic, in fact – not a matter of settled equivalences. 'I'll geld you, Lungs' he promises Face as a coda to his offer to make him keeper of his seraglio (II.ii.34). It is as if gelding, just a semitone down from gilding, were a form of decoration. And he relishes the prospect of walking naked between 'succubae' (II.ii.48) with no thought of the spiritual peril involved in copulating with she-devils. He produces the word as if it had no meaning other than its sound with its promise of fellatio and other sexual suckings.

We, of course, should be able to hear and understand what Mammon does not: the violence, the extravagance of his language are indices of his contrariness to nature. His desire to eat 'the swelling unctuous paps/Of a fat pregnant sow, newly cut off '(II.ii.83–4) – his own sensual paraphrase

---

[1] For a description of this *genre* see Brian Gibbons, *Jacobean City Comedy*, London, 1968, Appendix.

of a real Roman recipe – shows his opposition to life and fecundity at the same time as it expresses his rapacious, acquisitive enjoyment of them. Implicit in Jonson's characterisation through language is a moral commentary. But for all the affinities between this – and other 'city comedies' – and medieval morality drama,[1] the energy of this play's language is not primarily moralistic. Mammon, in his relish for language, is allied to the amorally magnanimous Lovewit who, though dramatically a *deus ex machina,* is revealed by his name to be the presiding genius of the play.

Mammon's love of wit expresses itself in overt applause. He exalts the menial 'Lungs' to the status of a classical nature deity – 'Zephyrus' – then asks if the 'bolt's head' 'Blushes'. Quick off the cue Face replies, 'Like a wench with child, sir,/That were, but now, discovered to her master'. 'Excellent witty Lungs!' comes Mammon's gratified response (II.ii.9–11). Face also engages Subtle in a metaphor match, capping Subtle in imagery as in all else:

> SUBTLE He looks in that deep ruff, like a head in a platter,
> Served in by a short cloak upon two trestles!
> FACE Or, what do you say to a collar of brawn, cut down
> Beneath the souse, and wriggled with a knife?   (IV.iii.24–7)[2]

One of the few anecdotes to link Jonson with Shakespeare relates that Shakespeare gave a spoon made of the alloy, latten, to one of Jonson's children as a christening gift. He then played on the consonance 'latten'/'Latin' and on Jonson's reputation as a classical scholar: 'Now you expect a great matter. But I shall give you a latten spoon, and you shall translate it' – presumably into some purer, more costly metal.[3] In *The Alchemist,* though the lead and iron brought to Face and Subtle remain steadfastly themselves, a transmutation of language is constantly at work. The word play – some of it silent as the cue for Dol on 'common' – by which one meaning is intended and another heard, subjects the language to the same kind of transformative poundings that the alchemist applies to his metals. L. A. Beaurline has written of Jonson's ability 'to vary, to press a matter to its greatest potential'.[4] He is describing Jonson's plotting but this economy – this pressing of finite materials into new combinations – is equally at work in Jonson's use of language. Surly, in his cod Spanish, speaks of *'la señora . . . como la bien aventuranza de mi vida.'* Face picks up, *'Mi vida?'* 'Slid, Subtle, he puts me in

---

[1] See Gibbons (op. cit.) for this subject; also Alan C. Dessen, '*The Alchemist:* Jonson's "Estates" Play', *Renaissance Drama,* vii (1964), pp. 35–54.

[2] Cf. the metaphor match between Hal and Falstaff in *Henry IV part i,* I.ii.71–9.

[3] *H.&S.,* vol. i, pp. 184–5; the quotation is from *Archdeacon Plume's Notes on Jonson.*

[4] L. A. Beaurline, *Jonson and Elizabethan Comedy,* San Marino, 1978, p. 203.

mind o' the widow' (IV.iii.61–3). Here dialogue, and also plot, are driven forward by an associative momentum. In an earlier scene Mammon and Face discuss the availability of 'stuff' on which to project:

> FACE   Buy
> The covering off o' churches.
> . . .
> Let 'em stand bare, as do their auditory.

From the idea of the hatless congregation comes the metaphor of churches with hats on:

> Or cap'em, new, with shingles.   (II.ii.13–16)

Subtle, basing his explanation of the alchemical process on the writings of Martin Delrio, describes the totality of substances as existing in an extended continuum:

> for 'twere absurd
> To think that nature, in the earth, bred gold
> Perfect, i' the instant. Something went before.
> There must be remote matter.   (II.iii.137–40)

This concept of a continuum in which some matter is 'remote', some near, is also implicit in several contemporary descriptions of verbal wit. See, for example, George Puttenham's account of the rhetorical figure *metalepsis*:

> which I call the *farfet,* as when we had rather fetch a word a great way off then to vse one nerer hand to expresse the matter aswel & plainer . . . leaping ouer the heads of a great many words, we take one that is furdest off, to vtter our matter by.[1]

Such 'leaping' is *not* what Subtle and Delrio have in mind. The alchemist's journey is more dogged:

> Nor can this remote matter, suddenly,
> Progress so from extreme, unto extreme,
> As to grow gold, and leap o'er all the means.

---

[1] George Puttenham, *The Arte of English Poesie*, ed. Gladys Doidge Willcock and Alice Walker, Cambridge, 1936, p. 183.

> Nature doth, first, beget th' imperfect; then
> Proceeds she to the perfect. (II.iii. 155–9)

But Mammon, who will buy rather than make the stone (II.ii.98–101) thinks of money as a way of abbreviating the alchemist's systematic route. Money acts like verbal wit, 'leaping over' intermediaries to fetch in what was remote. Samuel Johnson famously, and derogatively, defined wit as

> a kind of *discordia concurs*; a combination of dissimilar images, or discovery of occult resemblances in things apparently unlike . . . [in which] the most heterogeneous ideas are yoked by violence together. . .[1]

Mammon's rapacious purchase is an attempt at this kind of violence.

Nevertheless, the Italian poetic theorist, Emmanuele Tesauro, found a divine precedent for poetic wit in a God who 'dwells in the marshes and in the stars, and from the most sordid made the most divine of corporeal creatures'.[2] The wit of this lies in the abridgement of the gap between marshes and stars. Such a model might dignify the kind of social transformations which Subtle performs, 'translating' Face from the 'scarab' who picked over dunghills in search of clothes (I.i.34) to the more exalted 'suburb captain'. It is the parallel of the process which makes gold of metallic faeces (II.iii.62). This wit which exalts the base (and may equally debase the exalted) operates on every level of the play. Mammon's dialogue with Surly moves from the unironic mention of 'stout Marses . . . [and] . . . young Cupids' to the prostitutes of Pict-Hatch whose 'fire' is not only passion, but also inflammation and infection. But Surly sticks to Mammon's language, making the prostitutes the 'decayed Vestals . . . That keep the fire alive' (II.i.61–3). It is only by means of this metaphorical bridge that Mammon is then prompted to speak of infections.

Two divergent pressures – one towards diversity and fragmentation, the other towards unity, uniformity and identity – are operating on various levels in *The Alchemist*. Alchemy is itself predicated on the idea of the fundamental unity – not just continuity – of the material world. By transforming baser metals into the gold to which they aspire it is as if their 'true natures' were recovered. The neurologist Oliver Sacks, in describing the response to the anti-Parkinsonian drug L-Dopa, writes about the 'debased metaphysics' which looks for a miracle drug to 'restore' a lost state of

---

[1] from the life of Cowley in Samuel Johnson, *Lives of the English Poets*, ed. G. B. Hill, Oxford, 1905, vol. i, p. 20.

[2] Emmanuele Tesauro, *Il Cannocchiale Aristotelico*, Turin, 1670, p. 584; this passage is translated by S. L. Bethell in 'Gracian, Tesauro and the nature of Metaphysical Wit', in *Northern Miscellany*, i, 1953, p. 33.

perfect health and happiness – a golden age. 'Mysticism', he enlarges in a note, 'arises by taking analogy for identity – turning similes and metaphors (or 'as' statements) into absolutes (or 'is' statements), converting a useful epistemology into 'absolute truth'.[1] One can see such thinking, with its collapse of distinctions, in practice as Sir Epicure Mammon appropriates every myth available to him and reduces each to a description of alchemy:

> I'll show you a book, where Moses, and his sister,
> And Solomon have written, of the art;
> Ay, and a treatise penned by Adam . . .
> . . .
> . . . I have a piece of Jason's fleece, too,
> Which was no other, than a book of alchemy,
> . . .
> . . . this, th' Hesperian garden, Cadmus' story,
> Jove's shower, the boon of Midas, Argus' eyes,
> Boccace his Demogorgon, thousands more,
> All abstract riddles of our stone . . .   (II.i.81–3; 89–90; 101–4)

Sacks expands on the kind of mysticism – a 'mystical holism' – of which alchemy is an example:

> [it] asserts that the world is an entirely uniform and undifferentiated mass of 'world-stuff', 'primal matter', or plasm . . . The therapeutic correlate of such a monist mysticism is the notion of an all-purpose drug, a Panacea or Catholicon, a Quintessential extract of World-Stuff or Brain-Stuff, absolutely pure bottled Goodness or Godness (or Guinness) – de Quincey's 'portable ecstasy corked up in a pink-bottle'.[2]

Or the Philosopher's Stone?

The ur-matter on which the theory of alchemy is predicated is matched by the myth of an original language: the language used by Adam when he gave each creature its name; a language without universals in which every name is a proper name. For all the irrepressible verbal and idiomatic diversity in *The Alchemist* the play and its personnel do suggest the possibility of such an original language – whether the High German that some contemporary philologists had claimed for Adam (II.i.84) or the more traditional Hebrew (II.v.17). Subtle hints at the Adamic state in which every name is a proper name and every proper name is unique (a recipe for incomprehensibility) when he seems to identify Ananias with 'the varlet/That

[1] Oliver W. Sacks, *Awakenings*, Harmondsworth, 1976, p. 50.
[2] ibid., pp. 50–1.

cozened the Apostles' (II.v.72–3). The same may be said of Kastril's delighted response to Subtle's 'Pray God, your sister prove but pliant'. 'Why,/Her name is so' (IV.iv.89–90).

But the best-preserved and most communicative ancient language is the body language in which Dol is particularly fluent. She is urged to 'tickle [the Spaniard] with [her] mother-tongue' since 'His great/Verdugoship has not a jot of language' (III.iii.70–1). The couplings of sexual union are presented as a form of wit. Mammon, hot for Dol, asks if there is 'No means,/No trick, to give a man a taste of her – wit – /Or so?' (II.iii.258–60). And Lovewit, asking us to consider 'What a young wife, and a good brain may do' (V.v.155), suggests a kind of equation between sexual resourcefulness and more cerebral wit. The wit of sex – like the wit of money – lies in its power to abridge distances and unite the diverse.

Dol is the 'common wealth' of Face and Subtle; she is also their 'republic' (*res publica*: common thing) (I.i.110). The conflicting pressures – the one towards unity, concord and monoglossia, the other towards diversity, faction and jargon – have their political counterparts in the commonwealth to which the trio (and Mammon) aspire and the civil war to which their competitive individualism gives rise. The 'venture tripartite' between Dol, Face and Subtle declared 'All things in common./Without priority' (I.i.135–6). This egality is under strain at the outset of the play; by the end of Act II faction is entrenched.[1]

While ideas of commonwealth and civil war emerge in the play they are not its central concern. However, with hindsight it is possible to see the play casting a forward shadow across events in England thirty years later. It enables one to understand how Thomas Hobbes' fear of metaphor – his insistence upon settled significations – was of a piece with his horror of civil war:

> The Light of humane minds is Perspicuous Words, but by exact definitions first snuffed, and purged from ambiguity ... Metaphors, and senslesse and ambiguous words are like *ignes fatui*; and reasoning upon them, is wandering amongst innumerable absurdities; and their end, contention, and sedition, or contempt.[2]

But Hobbes can't keep metaphor out; the irony of 'snuffed' and *'ignes fatui'* may be mournful but it is not accidental. And in much of his work Hobbes' acquaintance Ben Jonson appears to celebrate (or at least indulge in) what he censures. But *The Alchemist,* with Lovewit as the presiding genius, is less censorious than most, and the wit which half-heartedly repairs the divisions

---

[1] See Note on Anabaptists, p. 19.
[2] *Leviathan*, ed. cit., pp. 116–17.

of language ('half-heartedly' because those divisions are what feed it) can make something even of stains – such as the 'poesies of the candle' which Lovewit finds on his ceiling (V.v.41).

PLOTTING AND STAGECRAFT

When we mean to build,
We first survey the plot, then draw the model,
And when we see the figure of the house,
Then must we rate the cost of the erection,
Which if we find outweighs ability,
What do we then but draw anew the model
In fewer offices, or at least desist
To build at all? Much more, in this great work –
Which is almost to pluck a kingdom down
And set another up – should we survey
The plot of situation and the model,
Consent upon a sure foundation,
Question surveyors, know our own estate,
How able such a work to undergo,
To weigh against his opposite.

(*Henry IV:2*, 1.iii.41–55)

Two kinds of plot are referred to in this speech by Shakespeare's Lord Bardolph; a third covertly. Ben Jonson had practical experience of all three. As a known Catholic, but also a known patriot, he earned the commission to seek out a Catholic priest with knowledge of the Gunpowder Plot. He was to give this priest safe conduct to the Lords where he would be expected to report on the conspiracy. Jonson was unable to find a priest ready to admit to such dangerous knowledge, but he did discover the flaw in the plot. There were too many involved. He reported that as many as 500 were 'enweaved' in the plot.[1] Leaks were inevitable.

Jonson also knew about that more ordinary kind of plotting with which Lord Bardolph illustrates his conspiracy theory. Whether or not Jonson underwent an apprenticeship to his step-father's trade of bricklaying, he was clearly able to follow the 'plots' or groundplans of houses – such as the one of his shop that Abel Drugger hands to Subtle in order to discover 'Which way [he] should make [his] door . . . And, where [his] shelves' (I.iii.11–12). Jonson applies a builder's constructive skills to his writing. See,

---

[1] *H.&S.*, vol. i, p. 41.

for example, his drystone-wall theory of syntax:

> The congruent, and harmonious fitting of parts in a sentence, hath almost the fastning, and force of knitting, and connexion: As in stones well squar'd, which will rise strong a great way without mortar.[1]

And Jonson knew about plotting plays (Shakespeare's covert metaphor in Lord Bardolph's speech). Coleridge thought *The Alchemist,* along with the *Oedipus Tyrannus* and *Tom Jones,* to be the three 'most perfect plots ever planned'.[2] *The Alchemist*'s plot is to some extent devised by its central characters – Dol, Subtle and Face – who are involved in a series of intersecting plots to defraud their willing gulls. But though the play comprises a series of mini-plots (conspiracies), the plot (temporal design) of the play is not coterminous with these. For Kenneth Tynan *The Alchemist* is 'a good episodic play . . . Like bead after bead the episodes click together upon the connecting string, which is chicanery and chiselry.'[3] But while the protagonists' plots are multiple, Jonson's plot is single. W. B. Yeats wrote that 'a poem comes right with a click like a closing box.'[4] And for all the lesser clicks which Tynan describes it is with such a single click that this play's plot closes: the click of a trap springing shut as the coney-catchers are caught. 'I am catched', says Face for whom there is nothing left but confession and the hope of a new bargain (V.iii.75). This is the moment at which Jonson's single plot overtakes the several plots of the trio. Face's face-saving lie to the colleagues he betrays – 'I sent for him, indeed' (V.iv. 129) – attempts to gloss over the fact that there was a move unforeseen by this master plotter.

An image of the play's momentum can be found in the progress of the supposed – though offstage – alchemical projection which Subtle feigns to be performing at Mammon's behest. It is a process of progressive elaboration and complication, culminating, not in the desired Philosopher's Stone, but in a noisy explosion (IV.v.55). Face's reaction at this point unknowingly foreshadows his genuine discomforture later when the unforeseen explodes:

> O sir, we are defeated! All the works
> Are flown *in fumo*: every glass is burst.
> Furnace, and all rent down! (IV.v.57–9)

---

[1] *H.&S.*, vol. viii, p. 623.

[2] *Coleridge's Table Talk and Omniana*, Oxford, 1917, p. 312.

[3] Kenneth Tynan, 'A Slamming of Doors' (1950) in R. V. Holdsworth, *Jonson: Every Man in his Humour and The Alchemist: A Casebook*, London, 1978, p. 224.

[4] *Letters on Poetry from W. B. Yeats to Dorothy Wellesley*, Oxford, 1964, p. 22.

Two scenes later he is to say in earnest 'We are undone, and taken' (IV.vii.114).

At the start of the play the various gulls (each of whom demands a different style of approach) file in, one or two at a time, allowing Face to change face and habit, Subtle to modify his tone, and Dol to switch as need calls from Fairy Queen to distracted gentlewoman. But this initially orderly and manageable sequence speeds up. The order quickens and becomes unpredictable, demanding more and more resourceful improvisation of the trio. At the play's half-way point (III.iii.) Face has returned from the Temple where Surly has failed to turn up, having instead arrived at the house disguised as the Spaniard whom Subtle now proposes to con with Dol's help. But just as Dol is about to 'tune her virginal' in readiness, Dapper turns up – late. Dol now has to dress as the Queen of Fairy and Subtle to get out of his alchemist's habit to become her priest. But no sooner is this underway than Drugger and Kastril arrive, eager to see, not the Priest of Fairy, but the 'Doctor'. Face now manages momentarily to clear the scene for Dapper's encounter with his 'aunt' by dispatching Kastril and Drugger in search of widow Pliant. But the fairy buzzing has barely started before Mammon's unexpected arrival demands a halt. Dapper is neutralised in desperate fashion – he is shoved in the privy with a gingerbread gag in his mouth.

Act IV begins with Mammon being hurried off with Dol who has stopped buzzing (and changed clothes) in order to spout Broughton while Face is left to cope with Kastril and his sister. But he has no time to change from alchemist's bellows-man (Mammon's friend 'Lungs') into the Captain Face that Kastril knows. Now he prays 'for a suit,/To fall . . ., like a curtain: flap' (IV.ii.6–7). But this is beyond even Face who is now put to the expert actor's test of having nothing – no prop – but himself with which to create the required illusion.

In the play's early scenes we take pleasure in the conspirators' control – in their ability to orchestrate events. As matters become more complicated and their gulls arrive late, early, not at all or unexpectedly, the pleasure we take is in watching their ability to improvise – as when Face brilliantly directs Kastril in his first practical quarrelling lesson, and then when Ananias turns up gives him too grounds to join in with theological denunciation, thus averting – by drowning out – the exposure which Surly is about to perform.

Jonson's language is so exciting and so various that a *reader* of this play might neglect its sheer *theatrical* brilliance. The pace and pitch of this play cannot be ignored in performance. Jonson's timing is impeccable – as when Ananias enters at the height of the uproar of the engineered quarrel with the words 'Peace to the household' (IV.vii.42). No auditor can ignore the noise that this play makes: the series of knocks, the explosion, the cry of the forgotten Dapper when his gingerbread gag has gone.

There are only two stage directions in the Quarto edition of *The Alchemist*: *Within* at II.i.25 and *Dol is seen* at II.iii.210 – the moment after Mammon has provided an inadvertent cue on 'common'. Such is the thrift of Jonson's writing that other stage directions are implicit and would be *discovered* by any full-witted actor in the course of performance. (For example 'Who's there?' [I.ii.162] clearly implies the direction – *One knocks without* – that Jonson added in Folio.) The several stage directions added to the Folio edition of the play clarify the situation for the reader but are, strictly speaking, superfluous. The economy of good stage writing demands that the actions be implicit in the words.

Thrift – making a little go a long way (no need to call Dol when 'common' has already been sounded) – is essential to good plotting; the Gunpowder Plot might have succeeded with fewer participants. Thrift is also necessary to the practical art of theatre. The Spanish costume which Drugger borrows from some actors pays its way like any worthy item in a theatre wardrobe – by adapting to a number of occasions. Whoever marries the widow must first 'become' the Spanish grandee by climbing into this costume. Like so much else in the play – Mammon's metalware, Dame Pliant herself – the range of this costume's potential is possessed and tried in fantasy before being finally realized by Lovewit.

This grandee's costume had an earlier life as a 'Hieronimo's cloak and hat'. Here is another link between Lovewit and his Blackfriars-dwelling creator, for Jonson is reputed to have played the part of Hieronimo in Kyd's *The Spanish Tragedy* (for which he also wrote additions). For all his professed loathing of the stuff and trumpery of theatrical shows, Jonson knew how to put them to use.

Note on Anabaptists

The Anabaptists whom Jonson satirizes with no trace of affection were, historically, egalitarians. During the occupation of Münster John of Leyden declared that 'all things were to be in common, there was to be no private property and nobody was to do any more work, but simply trust in God' (Norman Cohen, *The Pursuit of the Millenium*, London, 1957, p. 288). Leyden's ideal (which he contradicted by becoming a crowned tyrant) is very close to that expressed by the good Gonzalo in Shakespeare's *The Tempest*:

> I'th' commonwealth I would by contraries
> Execute all things; for no kind of traffic
> Would I admit; no name of magistrate;
> . . . .

> All things in common Nature should produce
> Without sweat or endeavour . . .   (II.i.143–5; 155–6)

For all Gonzalo's benignity, his companions are right to point out the flaw in his thinking – 'No sovereignty', he says, 'And yet he would be King'.

The Tempest was probably written shortly after *The Alchemist* and, with its magus protagonist, it looks at utopianism less cynically than does the earlier play to which Gonzalo's 'all things in common' may be a reference. But it is possibly informed, as *The Alchemist* certainly is, by the Anabaptist experiment in communal living.

Note on the Text

The Alchemist was first printed in quarto (Q) in 1612 and then included in the folio (F) edition of Jonson's *Works* in 1616. Jonson supervised the publication of both editions and it is likely that the copy text used for F was a corrected edition of Q. A second folio edition of the *Works* (F2) came out in 1640 and included some emendations. The present edition is based on F in all but a few details and all substantive variations from Q are recorded in the textual notes. Many of these variations stem from the tightening of regulations in the intervening years over the uttering of religious material on stage. Hence oaths which might be found blasphemous were emended in F to pagan or secular equivalents. For instance, 'God's will' (Q) becomes 'Death on me' in F (I.i.149). I have retained all these emendations (though there is a case for scrapping them) except one, at I.ii.56, which makes no sense outside the context of censorship.

Jonson's comprehensible punctuation in F has largely been retained, but spelling – except when the word was archaic or odd at the time – has been modernized. Jonson's liberal use of capitals and italics has been abandoned here – with some regret since the typography of F gives an edge to many words which, while not necessarily specialist, smack of jargon or restricted use. All editorial stage directions are in square brackets; any others are as in F. In F block entries of all participants precede each scene with the name of the first speaker at the beginning. Here entries are supplied as the action requires and all speech prefixes are ranged on the left. (Jonson distributes the prefixes within the line where a metrical line is shared by more than one character.)

FURTHER READING

Barton, Anne, *Ben Jonson, Dramatist*, Cambridge, 1984.

Barish, Jonas, *Ben Jonson and the Language of Prose Comedy*, Cambridge, Mass., 1960.

Beaurline, L. A., *Jonson and Elizabethan Comedy*, San Marino, 1978.

Blissett, W. and Van Fossen, R. W. edd., *A Celebration of Ben Jonson*, London 1973.

Craig, D. H., ed., *Ben Jonson: the Critical Heritage 1599–1798*, London, 1990.

Dessen, Alan C., 'The *Alchemist:* Jonson's "Estates" Play', *Renaissance Drama*, vii, 1964, pp. 35–54.

Duncan, Edgar Hill, 'Jonson's *Alchemist* and the Literature of Alchemy', *PMLA*, lxi, 1946, pp. 699–710.

Eliot, T. S., 'Ben Jonson', in *The Sacred Wood*, London, 1920.

Gibbons, Brian, *Jacobean City Comedy*, 1968, rev. ed., London, 1980.

Holdsworth, R. V., ed., *Jonson: Every Man in his Humour and The Alchemist: a Casebook*, London, 1978.

Hoy, Cyrus, 'The Pretended Piety of Jonson's *Alchemist*', *Renaissance Papers*, 1957, pp. 15–19.

Hyland, Peter, *Disguise and Role-Playing in Ben Jonson's Drama*, Salzburg, 1977.

Kay, W. David, *Ben Jonson: a Literary Life*, Basingstoke, 1995.

Kernan, Alvin, 'Alchemy and Acting: the Major Plays of Ben Jonson', in *Ben Jonson: Quadricentennial Essays*, ed. Mary Olive Thomas, Atlanta, 1973.

Knights, L. C., *Drama and Society in the Age of Jonson*, London, 1937.

Levin, Harry, 'Two Magian Comedies: *The Tempest* and *The Alchemist*', *Shakespeare Survey*, xxii, 1969, pp. 47–58.

Mebane, John S., *Renaissance Magic and the Return of the Golden Age*, Lincoln (Nebraska) and London, 1989. Chapter 7, 'The Renaissance Magus as Mock-Hero: Utopianism and Religious Enthusiasm in Ben Jonson's *The Alchemist*' was earlier published as an article in *Renaissance Drama*, x, 1979, pp. 117–139.

Miles, Rosalind, *Ben Jonson: his Crafts and Art*, London, 1990.

Partridge, E. B., *The Broken Compass*, London 1958.

Riggs, David, *Ben Jonson: A Life*, Cambridge, Mass., 1989.

Roberts, Gareth, *The Mirror of Alchemy: Alchemical Ideas and Images in Manuscripts and Books*, London, 1994.

Sweeney, John G., *Jonson and the Psychology of Public Theater*, Princetown, 1985.

Watson, Robert N., *Ben Jonson's Parodic Strategy*, Cambridge, Mass., 1987.

Womack, Peter, *Ben Jonson*, Oxford, 1986.

ABBREVIATIONS

F   *The Works of Benjamin Jonson*, London, 1616

F2   *The Works of Benjamin Jonson*, London, 1640

H.&S.   *Ben Jonson*, ed. C. H. Herford, P. & E. Simpson, 11 vols., Oxford, 1925–52

OED   *The Oxford English Dictionary*

Q   *The Alchemist*, London, 1612

T.C.B.   *Theatrum Chemicum Britannicum,* ed. Elias Ashmole, London, 1652

THE
ALCHEMIST.

A Comœdie.

Acted in the yeere 1610. By the
Kings Maiesties
Seruants.

The Author B. I.

Lvcret.

———petere inde coronam,
vnde priùs nulli velarint tempora Musæ.

LONDON,

Printed by WILLIAM STANSBY

M. DC. XVI.

[23]

TO THE LADY, MOST DESERVING HER NAME, AND BLOOD:
Mary,

LADY WROTH   5

MADAM,

In the age of sacrifices, the truth of religion was not in the
greatness, and fat of the offerings, but in the devotion, and zeal
of the sacrificers: else, what could a handful of gums have done
in the sight of a hecatomb? Or, how might I appear at this altar,   10
except with those affections, that no less love the light and
witness, than they have the conscience of your virtue? If what I
offer bear an acceptable odour, and hold the first strength, it is your
value of it, which remembers, where, when, and to whom it was
kindled. Otherwise, as the times are, there comes rarely forth that   15
thing, so full of authority, or example, but by assiduity and custom,
grows less, and loses. This, yet, safe in your judgment (which is a
Sidney's) is forbidden to speak more; lest it talk, or look like one of
the ambitious faces of the time: who, the more they paint, are the less
themselves.   20

> Your Ladyship's true honourer,
> Ben Jonson.

2–3   *DESERVING . . . BLOOD* most aequall with vertue, and her Blood: The Grace, and Glory of women Q

4–5   *Mary,* LADY WROTH daughter of Robert Sidney, first Earl of Leicester, and niece of Sir Philip Sidney; she married Sir Robert Wroth in 1604. The name was also spelled 'Worth' — hence 'deserving her name'

7–12   from Seneca, *De Beneficiis,* i.vi.2

9   *gums* incense

10   *hecatomb* huge public sacrifice

10–12   *Or, how . . . virtue?* Or how, yet, might a grateful minde be furnish'd against the iniquitie of Fortune; except, when she fail'd it, it had power to impart it selfe? A way found out, to ouercome euen those, whom Fortune hath enabled to returne most, since they, yet leaue themselues more. In this assurance am I planted; and stand with those affections at this Altar, as shall no more auoide the light and witnesse, then they do the conscience of your vertue Q

12   *conscience* consciousness

14   *value of it, which* valew, that Q

15   *as the times are* in these times Q

16   *assiduity* daylinesse Q

17   *This, yet* But this Q

19   *paint* use make up

TO THE READER

If thou beest more, thou art an understander, and then I trust thee. If
thou art one that takest up, and but a pretender, beware at what hands
thou receivest thy commodity; for thou wert never more fair in the way
to be cozened (than in this age) in poetry, especially in plays: wherein,
now, the concupiscence of jigs and dances so reigneth, as to run away   5
from nature, and be afraid of her, is the only point of art that tickles
the spectators. But how out of purpose, and place, do I name art? When
the professors are grown so obstinate contemners of it, and presumers
on their own naturals, as they are deriders of all diligence that way, and,
by simple mocking at the terms, when they understand not the things,   10
think to get off wittily with their ignorance. Nay, they are esteemed the
more learned, and sufficient for this, by the multitude, through their
excellent vice of judgment. For they commend writers, as they do
fencers, or wrestlers; who if they come in robustiously, and put for it
with a great deal of violence, are received for the braver fellows: when   15
many times their own rudeness is the cause of their disgrace, and a little touch of their adversary gives all that boisterous force the foil. I deny
not, but that these men, who always seek to do more than enough, may
some time happen on something that is good, and great; but very sel-
dom: and when it comes it doth not recompense the rest of their ill. It   20
sticks out perhaps, and is more eminent, because all is sordid, and vile
about it: as lights are more discerned in a thick darkness, than a faint
shadow. I speak not this, out of a hope to do good on any man, against
his will; for I know, if it were put to the question of theirs, and mine,
the worse would find more suffrages: because the most favour com-   25
mon errors. But I give thee this warning, that there is a great difference
between those, that (to gain the opinion of copie) utter all they can,
however unfitly; and those that use election, and a mean. For it is only
the disease of the unskilful, to think rude things greater than polished:
or scattered more numerous than composed.   30

This preface is taken from the British Library Q. It was not included in F
A more expanded version of these views (which derive from Quintilian) can be found
in Jonson's *Discoveries* (*H. & S*.viii, esp. pp. 583, 586–7)
 1 *To the Reader . . . than composed* Q; not in F
   more i.e. more than a reader
 9 *naturals* what nature has given them (with a pun on 'fools')
 15 *braver* finer
 27 *copie* copiousness   *all they can* all they know (ken)
 28 *those that use election, and a mean* those that employ discrimination and moderation

THE PERSONS OF THE PLAY

SUBTLE, *The Alchemist*
FACE, *The Housekeeper*
DOL COMMON,
Their Colleague
DAPPER, *A Clerk*
DRUGGER, *A Tobaccoman*
LOVEWIT, *Master of the House*

EPICURE MAMMON,
A Knight
SURLY, *A Gamester*
TRIBULATION, *A Pastor*
of Amsterdam
ANANIAS, *A Deacon there*
KASTRIL, *The Angry Boy*
DAME PLIANT,
His Sister: A Widow

Neighbours
Officers
Mutes

The Scene

LONDON [, inside Lovewit's house and in the street outside]

---

1 *play* Comoedie Q
6 *Tobaccoman* tobacco was a new and fashionable commodity and tobacco sellers a new
   breed of tradesmen. See John Earle, *Microcosmography* (1628) for the 'character' of *A
   Tobacco Seller*
   Kastril an obsolete spelling of 'kestril'. As an 'angry boy' he is one of a type of pugnacious
   men about town
   Mutes non-speaking parts, e.g. the Parson of V.v. 118
17 The Scene *LONDON* F; not in Q

[26]

THE ALCHEMIST

The Argument

T   he sickness hot, a master quit, for fear,
H   is house in town: and left one servant there.
E   ase him corrupted, and gave means to know
A   cheater, and his punk; who, now brought low,
L   eaving their narrow practice, were become   5
C   ozeners at large: and, only wanting some
H   ouse to set up, with him they here contract,
E   ach for a share, and all begin to act.
M   uch company they draw, and much abuse,
I   n casting figures, telling fortunes, news,   10
S   elling of flies, flat bawdry, with the stone:
T   ill it, and they, and all in fume are gone.

---

1 *sickness* plague
4 *punk* whore
10 *casting figures* drawing up horoscopes
11 *stone* the Philosopher's Stone
12 *fume* smoke

[27]

PROLOGUE

Fortune, that favours fools, these two short hours
    We wish away; both for your sakes, and ours,
Judging spectators: and desire in place,
    To th'author justice, to ourselves but grace.
Our scene is London, 'cause we would make known,   5
    No country's mirth is better than our own,
No clime breeds better matter, for your whore,
    Bawd, squire, imposter, many persons more,
Whose manners, now called humours, feed the stage:
    And which have still been subject, for the rage   10
Or spleen of comic writers. Though this pen
    Did never aim to grieve, but better men;
Howe'er the age, he lives in, doth endure
    The vices that she breeds, above their cure.
But, when the wholesome remedies are sweet,   15
    And, in their working, gain, and profit meet,
He hopes to find no spirit so much diseased,
    But will, with such fair correctives be pleased.
For here, he doth not fear, who can apply.
    If there be any, that will sit so nigh   20
Unto the stream, to look what it doth run,
    They shall find things, they'd think, or wish, were done;
They are so natural follies, but so shown.
    As even the doers may see, and yet not own.

---

7 *for* William Empson observes that this must mean 'as providing' and not 'because' ('The Alchemist and the Critics', 1970, in *Casebook* ed. R. V. Holdsworth)

8 *squire* pimp

9 *now called humours* according to medieval psychologists an individual's temperament was determined by the balance and proportion of four bodily humours: blood, phlegm, red bile and black bile. These in turn reflect the balance of the four elements: air, water, fire and earth. A 'humour' thence came to mean any bent of personality. Jonson protests against the misuse of this term (as an excuse for fashionably interesting foibles) in his induction to *Every Man Out of his Humour*, 110–17

10 *for* to Q

12 *better* a verb

19 *apply* interpret veiled allusions

The Alchemist

Act I, Scene i

[Inside Lovewit's house]

[Enter] FACE, SUBTLE, DOL COMMON

FACE
 Believ't, I will.
SUBTLE   Thy worst. I fart at thee.
DOL
 Ha' you your wits? Why gentlemen! For love–
FACE
 Sirrah, I'll strip you—
SUBTLE   What to do? Lick figs
 Out at my—
FACE   Rogue, rogue, out of all your sleights.
DOL
 Nay, look ye! Sovereign, General, are you madmen?   5
SUBTLE
 O, let the wild sheep loose.

                                        [threatens FACE *with phial]*
                         I'll gum your silks
 With good strong water, an' you come.
DOL   Will you have
 The neighbours hear you? Will you betray all?
 Hark, I hear somebody.
FACE   Sirrah—
SUBTLE   I shall mar
 All that the tailor has made, if you approach.   10
FACE
 You most notorious whelp, you insolent slave
 Dare you do this?
SUBTLE   Yes faith, yes faith.
FACE   Why! Who
 Am I, my mongrel? Who am I?
SUBTLE   I'll tell you,
 Since you know not yourself—

---

 3 *figs* piles, the *ficus morbus*
 6 *gum* stiffen
 10 *All that the tailor has made* this establishes that Face's persona has been manufactured

FACE   Speak lower, rogue.

SUBTLE

Yes. You were once (time's not long past) the good,   15
Honest, plain, livery-three-pound-thrum; that kept
Your master's worship's house, here, in the Friars,
For the vacations—

FACE   Will you be so loud?

SUBTLE

Since, by my means, translated suburb-Captain.

FACE

By your means, Doctor Dog?

SUBTLE   Within man's memory,   20
All this, I speak of.

FACE   Why, I pray you, have I
Been countenanced by you? Or you, by me?
Do but collect, sir, where I met you first.

SUBTLE

  I do not hear well.

FACE   Not of this, I think it.
But I shall put you in mind, sir, at Pie Corner,   25
Taking your meal of steam in, from cooks' stalls,
Where, like the father of hunger, you did walk
Piteously costive, with your pinched-horn-nose,
And your complexion, of the Roman wash,
Stuck full of black, and melancholic worms,   30
Like powder corns, shot, at th'artillery-yard.

16 *livery-three-pound-thrum* 'livery' is a servant's garb, 'three-pound' is probably Face's
    annual wage, and 'thrum' is waste thread – the loose end of a weaver's warp. The whole
    compound suggests that Face was a lowly menial.
17 *the Friars* Blackfriars in London, between St. Paul's and the river; site of the Blackfriars
    theatre and also of Jonson's home for a time
18 *vacations* between the four terms of the Law-Courts: Hilary (11th–31st January), Easter
    (mid-April–8th May), Trinity (22nd May–12th June), and Michaelmas (2nd–25th
    November). There was a lull in London activity during vacations
19 *translated* transformed into
23 *collect* recollect
25 *Pie Corner* a place in nearby Smithfield, noted for cooks' shops
26 *Taking your meal of steam in* Martial I.xcii. 7–10
27 *father of hunger* Catullus xxi. 1. 'pater esuritionum'
29 *of the Roman wash* a 'wash' is a dye. The Roman wash may be dark like an Italian, or red
    like the Scarlet Whore of Babylon, as the Roman church was portrayed
31 *powder corns* grains of gunpowder
    artillery-yard the exercise yard of the Honourable Artillery Company at Teasel Close
    (now Artillery Lane). It was also used by the City Trainband (a home guard)

SUBTLE

    I wish, you could advance your voice, a little.

FACE

    When you went pinned up, in the several rags
    You'd raked, and picked from dunghills, before day,
    Your feet in mouldy slippers, for your kibes,   35
    A felt of rug, and a thin threaden cloak,
    That scarce would cover your no-buttocks—

SUBTLE   So, sir!

FACE

    When all your alchemy, and your algebra,
    Your minerals, vegetals, and animals,
    Your conjuring, cozening, and your dozen of trades,   40
    Could not relieve your corps, with so much linen
    Would make you tinder, but to see a fire;
    I ga' you countenance, credit for your coals,
    Your stills, your glasses, your materials,
    Built you a furnace, drew you customers   45
    Advanced all your black arts; lent you, beside,
    A house to practise in—

SUBTLE   Your master's house?

FACE

    Where you have studied the more thriving skill
    Of bawdry, since.

SUBTLE   Yes, in your master's house.
    You, and the rats, here, kept possession.   50
    Make it not strange. I know, y'were one, could keep
    The buttr'y-hatch still locked, and save the chippings,
    Sell the dole-beer to aqua-vitae-men,
    The which, together with your Christmas vails,
    At post and pair, your letting out of counters,   55

---

  35 *kibes* chilblains
36–7 see Martial I.xcii, 7–8
  36 *felt of rug* rough wool hat   *threaden* made of thread
  39 *vegetals* vegetable substances
  41 *corps* body
  52 *butt'ry-hatch* the buttery was where drink was stored
  53 *aqua-vitae-men* liquor dealers
  54 *Christmas vails* Christmas boxes, tips
  55 *post and pair* a card game
      letting out of counters as in roulette now, counters (then usually metal) were used in place
      of coin for gambling. Face would be tipped for supplying these

Made you a pretty stock, some twenty marks,
And gave you credit, to converse with cobwebs,
Here, since your mistress' death hath broke up house.

FACE

You might talk softlier, rascal.

SUBTLE   No, you scarab,
I'll thunder you, in pieces. I will teach you   60
How to beware, to tempt a fury again
That carries tempest in his hand, and voice.

FACE

The place has made you valiant.

SUBTLE   No, your clothes.
Thou vermin, have I ta'en thee, out of dung,
So poor, so wretched, when no living thing   65
Would keep thee company, but a spider, or worse?
Raised thee from brooms, and dust, and wat'ring-pots?
Sublimed thee, and exalted thee, and fixed thee
I' the third region, called our state of grace?
Wrought thee to spirit, to quintessence, with pains   70
Would twice have won me the philosopher's work?
Put thee in words, and fashion? Made thee fit
For more than ordinary fellowships?
Given thee thy oaths, thy quarrelling dimensions?
Thy rules, to cheat at horse-race, cock-pit, cards,   75
Dice, or whatever gallant tincture else?
Made thee a second, in mine own great art?
And have I this for thank? Do you rebel?

59   *scarab* dung beetle
68   *Sublimed* converted into vapour to remove impurities
     exalted alchemical exaltation is a process of purification and concentration
     fixed stabilized
69   *third region* the upper, and purest, region of the air
     our state of grace the high state of grace Q
70   *quintessence* the 'fifth essence' of which heavenly bodies are composed and which is latent
     in substances composed of the four material elements
71   *philosopher's work* Philosopher's Stone
72–4 *Put thee ... dimensions* taught you how to speak and dress; enabled you to enter company
     a) better than average b) beyond what you would find at cheap eating houses (ordinaries);
     taught you how to swear and on what grounds you may quarrel
75   *cock-pit* cock-fighting
76   *gallant tincture* touch of gallantry; *tincture* is an alchemical term

Do you fly out, i' the projection?
Would you be gone, now?
DOL   Gentlemen, what mean you?   80
Will you mar all?
SUBTLE   Slave, thou hadst had no name—
DOL
Will you undo yourselves, with civil war?
SUBTLE
Never been known, past *equi clibanum*,
The heat of horse-dung, under ground, in cellars,
Or an ale-house, darker than deaf John's: been lost   85
To all mankind, but laundresses, and tapsters,
Had not I been.
DOL   Do you know who hears you, Sovereign?
FACE
Sirrah—
DOL   Nay, General, I thought you were civil—
FACE
I shall turn desperate, if you grow thus loud.
SUBTLE
And hang thyself, I care not.
FACE   Hang thee, collier,   90
And all thy pots, and pans, in picture I will,
Since thou hast moved me—
DOL   (O, this'll o'erthrow all.)
FACE
Write thee up bawd, in Paul's; have all thy tricks
Of coz'ning with a hollow coal, dust, scrapings,

---

79 *projection* the moment of alchemical transformation when the Philosopher's Stone
    interpenetrates qualities with the matter to be changed
83 *equi clibanum* lit. 'horse's oven' – horse dung was used by alchemists when a moderate
    heat was desired
85 *deaf John's* an alehouse (unidentified)
90 *Hang thee, collier* cf. *Twelfth Night* III.iv.119, 'Hang him, foul collier!' (of the devil). It was
    commonplace to associate colliers with the infernal. Subtle's smoky appearance would
    suggest the remark
91 *in picture* Face threatens to expose Subtle with a public advertisement
93 *Paul's* St. Paul's Cathedral (not the one now standing); a popular meeting place for secular
    purposes of social and business exchange. In Dekker's *The Dead Tearme* (1608) Paul's
    steeple complains 'am I like a common Mart where all Commodities . . . are to be bought
    and solde' (E^r)
94 *cozening with a hollow coal* Chaucer describes this trick in the *Canon's Yeoman's Tale*,
    1159–64. Silver filings are placed inside a hollow coal which is then sealed with wax. When

Searching for things lost, with a sieve, and shears,   95
Erecting figures, in your rows of houses,
And taking in of shadows, with a glass,
Told in red letters: and a face, cut for thee,
Worse than Gamaliel Ratsey's.

DOL   Are you sound?
Ha' you your senses, masters?

FACE   I will have   100
A book, but barely reckoning thy impostures,
Shall prove a true philosopher's stone, to printers.

SUBTLE
Away, you trencher-rascal.

FACE   Out you dog-leech,
The vomit of all prisons—

DOL   Will you be
Your own destructions, gentlemen?

FACE   Still spewed out   105
For lying too heavy o' the basket.

SUBTLE   Cheater

FACE
Bawd.

SUBTLE Cow-herd.

FACE   Conjurer.

SUBTLE   Cut purse.

FACE   Witch.

DOL   O me!
We are ruined! Lost! Ha' you no more regard
To your reputations? Where's your judgment? S'light,

---

the wax melts molten silver appears amongst the coals to convince prospective clients
  of the 'alchemist's' prowess
95 *sieve, and shears* the points of shears are stuck into the rim of a sieve to form a dowsing
  instrument for divination
96 *erecting figures* see *Argument* 10
97 *glass* a crystal or beryl ball which is supposedly entered by angels which can be discerned
  and understood by a *speculatrix*
98 *red letters: and a face, cut for thee* eye-catching rubric headings and a wood-cut portrait
99 *Gamaliel Ratsey* a highwayman, hanged in 1605. He worked in a hideous mask, probably
  referred to here
103 *trencher-rascal* meal-scrounger
104 *dog-leech* dog-doctor (i.e. quack)
106 *For lying too heavy o' the basket* for taking an unfairly large helping from the communal
  basket of scraps for prisoners
109 *'Slight* 'God's light'

Have yet, some care of me, o' your republic— 110

FACE

Away this brach. I'll bring thee, rogue, within
The statute of sorcery, *tricesimo tertio*,
Of Harry the Eighth: ay, and (perhaps) thy neck
Within a noose, for laund'ring gold, and barbing it.

DOL

You'll bring your head within a coxcomb, will you? 115
    She catcheth out Face his sword: and breaks Subtle's glass
And you, sir, with your menstrue, gather it up.
S'death, you abominable pair of stinkards,
Leave off your barking, and grow one again,
Or, by the light that shines, I'll cut your throats.
I'll not be made a prey unto the marshal, 120
For ne'er a snarling dog-bolt o' you both.
Ha' you together cozened all this while,
And all the world, and shall it now be said
You've made most courteous shift, to cozen yourselves?
[*To* FACE] You will accuse him? You will bring him in 125
Within the statute? Who shall take your word?
A whoreson, upstart, apocryphal captain,
Whom not a puritan, in Blackfriars, will trust
So much, as for a feather! [*To* SUBTLE] And you, too,
Will give the cause, forsooth? You will insult, 130
And claim a primacy, in the divisions?

---

110 *republic* Lat. 'common thing', i.e. Dol

111 *brach* bitch

112–13 *tricesimo tertio . . . Eighth* this act (classified as 33 Henry VIII c.8) was passed in 1541 and forbade, *inter alia*, invocations to find gold or silver and divinations to discover lost or stolen goods. It was repealed in 1863

114 *laundering . . . barbing* washing gold coins in acid to dissolve some of the surface was known as 'laundering'; 'barbing' involved clipping the edges. Tampering with coin was a capital offence
    it not in Q

115 *You'll bring your head . . . you?* you're determined to be a fool? The coxcomb (which Dol counterposes to the noose [114]) was the traditional fool's headdress

116 *menstrue* solvent

120 *marshal* provost-marshal, in charge of prisons

121 *dog-bolt* a blunt-headed arrow. Here used figuratively and with an associative logic from 'snarling'

127 *apocryphal* fictional

128–9 *Blackfriars . . . feather!* many Puritans lived in Blackfriars. Surprisingly they were the principal purveyors of feathers and plumes – a fact that let them in for much satire

You must be chief? As if you, only, had
The powder to project with? And the work
Were not begun out of equality?
The venture tripartite? All things in common?   135
Without priority? 'Sdeath, you perpetual curs,
Fall to your couples again, and cozen kindly,
And heartily, and lovingly, as you should,
And lose not the beginning of a term,
Or, by this hand, I shall grow factious too,   140
And take my part, and quit you.

FACE   'Tis his fault,
He ever murmurs, and objects his pains,
And says, the weight of all lies upon him.

SUBTLE
Why, so it does.

DOL   How does it? Do not we
Sustain our parts?

SUBTLE   Yes, but they are not equal.   145

DOL
Why, if your part exceed today, I hope
Ours may, tomorrow, match it.

SUBTLE   Ay, they may.

DOL
May, murmuring mastiff? Ay, and do. Death on me!
Help me to throttle him.

SUBTLE   Dorothy, mistress Dorothy,
'Ods precious, I'll do anything. What do you mean?   150

DOL
Because o' your fermentation, and cibation?

SUBTLE
Not I, by heaven—

DOL   Your Sol, and Luna—[*To* FACE] help me.

---

133   *powder to project with* here used figuratively for criminal inventiveness
136   *'Sdeath* 'God's death'
137   *couples* the word used for a pair of hunting dogs working together
      cozen kindly deceive amicably (with a pun on 'act like relatives')
139   *term* of the law courts. The four terms were periods of great business and social activity
      and provided opportunities for swindlers
142   *objects* 'puts forward' (a Latinism)
148   *Death on me* Gods will Q
150   *'Ods precious* 'God's precious [blood]'
151   *fermentation . . . cibation* the sixth and seventh processes of alchemy
152   *Sol, and Luna* gold and silver; each metal was associated with a planet

SUBTLE
Would I were hanged then. I'll conform myself.

DOL
Will you, sir, do so then, and quickly: swear.

SUBTLE
What should I swear?

DOL   To leave your faction, sir.   155
And labour, kindly, in the common work.

SUBTLE
Let me not breathe, if I meant ought, beside.
I only used those speeches, as a spur
To him.

DOL   I hope we need no spurs, sir. Do we?

FACE
'Slid, prove today, who shall shark best.

SUBTLE   Agreed.   160

DOL
Yes, and work close, and friendly.

SUBTLE   'Slight, the knot
Shall grow the stronger, for this breach, with me.

DOL
Why so, my good baboons! Shall we go make
A sort of sober, scurvy, precise neighbours,
(That scarce have smiled twice, sin' the king came in)   165
A feast of laughter, at our follies? Rascals,
Would run themselves from breath, to see me ride,
Or you t'have but a hole, to thrust your heads in,
For which you should pay ear-rent? No, agree.
And may Don Provost ride a-feasting, long,   170
In his old velvet jerkin, and stained scarves

---

155 *faction* quarrel
160 *'Slid* 'God's [eye] lid'
     shark swindle
164 *sort of* set of
     precise puritanical; strict in religious observance
165 *sin' the king came in* i.e. since 1603
167–9 *to see . . . ear-rent* to see me displayed in a cart as a prostitute and you pilloried and your
     ears cut off. (Dee's assistant Kelley lost both ears as a punishment for coining)
170 *Don Provost* Provost-marshal 'who is often both Informer, Judge, and Executioner . . .
     [and] punishes disorderlie Souldiors, Coyners, Free-booters, highway robbers . . .' Cotgrave,
     A Dictionary of the French and English Tongues, London, 1611. Dol here evokes the
     hangman, entitled to the clothes of his victims

(My noble Sovereign, and worthy General)
Ere we contribute a new crewel garter
To his most worsted worship.

SUBTLE   Royal Dol!
Spoken like Claridiana, and thy self!   175

FACE
For which, at supper, thou shalt sit in triumph,
And not be styled Dol Common, but Dol Proper,
Dol Singular: the longest cut, at night,
Shall draw thee for his Dol Particular.   [*A bell rings*]

SUBTLE
Who's that? One rings. To the window, Dol. Pray heaven,   180
The master do not trouble us, this quarter.

FACE
O, fear not him. While there dies one, a week,
O'the plague, he's safe, from thinking toward London.
Beside, he's busy at his hop-yards, now:
I had a letter from him. If he do,   185
He'll send such word, for airing o' the house
As you shall have sufficient time, to quit it:
Though we break up a fortnight, 'tis no matter.

SUBTLE
Who is it, Dol?

DOL   A fine young quodling.

FACE   O,
My lawyer's clerk, I lighted on, last night,   190
In Holborn, at the Dagger. He would have
(I told you of him) a familiar,
To rifle with, at horses, and win cups.

173–4 *crewel garter . . . worsted worship* two puns playing on 'crewel' (yarn and 'cruel') and
       'worsted' (dressed in worsted and 'thwarted')
  175 *Claridiana* heroine of Diego Ortuñez del Calahorra's *Caballero del Sol*, a popular romance
       first translated as *The Mirror of Princely Deeds and Knighthood*, 1578
177–9 *Common . . . Proper . . . Singular . . . Particular* grammatical categories used to indicate
       Dol's sexual range
  178 *longest cut* they will draw straws for Dol
  189 *quodling* an unripe apple; youth
  191 *Dagger* the Dagger tavern was famous for pies and frumety. It was perhaps also a gambling
       house
  192 *familiar* spirit
  193 *rifle* gamble (raffle)

DOL

O, let him in.

SUBTLE   Stay. Who shall do't?

FACE   Get you

Your robes on. I will meet him, as going out.   195

DOL

And what shall I do?

FACE   Not be seen, away.

Seem you very reserved.   [*Exit* DOL]

SUBTLE   Enough.   [*Exit* SUBTLE]

FACE   God be w'you, sir.

I pray you, let him know that I was here.

His name is Dapper. I would gladly have stayed, but—

Act I, Scene ii

DAPPER [*within*]

Captain, I am here.

FACE   Who's that? He's come, I think, Doctor.

[*Enter* DAPPER]

Good faith, sir, I was going away.

DAPPER   In truth,

I am very sorry, Captain.

FACE   But I thought

Sure, I should meet you.

DAPPER   Ay, I am very glad.

I had a scurvy writ, or two, to make,   5

And I had lent my watch last night, to one

That dines, today, at the sheriff's: and so was robbed

Of my pass-time.

[*Enter* SUBTLE *in doctor's robes*]

Is this the cunning-man?

FACE

This is his worship.

DAPPER   Is he a Doctor?

FACE   Yes.

6 *watch* a desirable status-commodity

DAPPER
   And ha' you broke with him, Captain?
FACE   Ay.
DAPPER   And how?   10
FACE
   Faith, he does make the matter, sir, so dainty,
   I know not what to say—
DAPPER   Not so, good Captain.
FACE
   Would I were fairly rid on't, believe me.
DAPPER
   Nay, now you grieve me, sir. Why should you wish so?
   I dare assure you. I'll not be ungrateful.   15
FACE
   I cannot think you will, sir. But the law
   Is such a thing—and then, he says, Read's matter
   Falling so lately—
DAPPER   Read? He was an ass,
   And dealt, sir, with a fool.
FACE   It was a clerk, sir.
DAPPER
   A clerk?
FACE   Nay, hear me, sir, you know the law   20
   Better, I think—
DAPPER   I should, sir, and the danger.
   You know I showed the statute to you?
FACE   You did so.
DAPPER
   And will I tell, then? By this hand, of flesh,
   Would it might never write good court-hand, more,
   If I discover. What do you think of me,   25

10 *broke* broached the matter
11 *he does . . . dainty* he treats it with such fastidious caution
17 *Read's matter* in 1608 Simon Read, a Southwark doctor, was given a pardon for having
    (in November 1607) invoked three spirits in order to discover a thief
19 *a fool* presumably Tobias Matthews who had been robbed and called upon Read's
    assistance
22 *the statute* see I.i.112
24 *court-hand* a much abbreviated (and therefore hard to read) style of writing used in the
    law courts
25 *discover* reveal

That I am a *Chiause*?

FACE   What's that?

DAPPER   The Turk was, here—

As one would say, do you think I am a Turk?

FACE

I'll tell the Doctor so.

DAPPER   Do, good sweet Captain.

FACE

Come, noble Doctor, 'pray thee, let's prevail,

This is the gentleman, and he is no *Chiause*.   30

SUBTLE

Captain, I have returned you all my answer.

I would do much, sir, for your love—but this

I neither may, nor can.

FACE   Tut, do not say so.

You deal, now, with a noble fellow, Doctor,

One that will thank you, richly, and he's no *Chiause*:   35

Let that, sir, move you.

SUBTLE   Pray you, forbear—

FACE   He has

Four angels, here—

SUBTLE   You do me wrong, good sir.

FACE

Doctor, wherein? To tempt you, with these spirits?

SUBTLE

To tempt my art, and love, sir, to my peril.

'Fore heaven, I scarce can think you are my friend,   40

That so would draw me to apparent danger.

FACE

I draw you? A horse draw you, and a halter,

You, and your flies together—

DAPPER   Nay, good Captain.

---

26 *Chiause* in July 1607 a Turk named Mustafa arrived in England declaring himself
   ambassador from the Sultan, though he used only the title 'Chaush' (messenger). The
   Levant merchants were fooled into entertaining him at great cost and 'to play the Chaush
   . . . seems to have become a popular synonym for imposture'. *The Travels of Sir John
   Sanderson in the Levant*, ed. Sir W. Foster, London, 1931, p. xxxv

37 *angels* gold coins bearing a picture of the Archangel Michael combatting a dragon. The
   word – conjoining the spiritual and the pecuniary – was much played upon, as here

38 *spirits* continues the play on 'angels'

42 *a horse draw you* i.e. in a cart to be hanged

FACE

That know no difference of men.

SUBTLE   Good words, sir.

FACE

Good deeds, sir, Doctor Dogs-meat. 'Slight I bring you   45
No cheating Clim o' the Cloughs, or Claribels,
That look as big as five-and-fifty, and flush,
And spit out secrets, like hot custard—

DAPPER   Captain.

FACE

Nor any melancholic under-scribe,
Shall tell the Vicar: but, a special gentle,   50
That is the heir to forty marks, a year,
Consorts with the small poets of the time,
Is the sole hope of his old grandmother,
That knows the law, and writes you six fair hands,
Is a fine clerk, and has his cyph'ring perfect,   55
Will take his oath, o' the Greek Testament
If need be, in his pocket: and can court
His mistress, out of Ovid.

DAPPER   Nay, dear Captain.

FACE

Did you not tell me, so?

DAPPER   Yes, but I'd ha' you
Use master Doctor, with some more respect.   60

FACE

Hang him proud stag, with his broad velvet head.

---

45 *Dogs-meat* Dogges-mouth Q
46 *Clim o' the Cloughs . . . Claribels* Clim of the Clough, 'an archer good ynough' (*Ballad of Adam Bell*) and an outlaw. Nashe uses his name for the devil in *Pierce Pennilesse* (1592). Sir Claribel pursues the False Florimell in Spenser's *Faerie Queene* IV.ix
47 *as big as five-and-fifty, and flush* all 55 cards in the same suit – an unbeatable hand in Primero
50 *Vicar* vicar general, acting for the bishop in ecclesiastical courts
     gentle gentleman
54 *six fair hands* six styles of handwriting; probably those cited in John de Beau Chesne and John Baildon's *A Booke containing divers sortes of hands, as well the English as French secretarie with the Italian, Roman, Chancelry & Court hands*, London, 1571
55 *cyphering* book-keeping
56 *Testament* this is the Q reading; in F it is changed to 'Xenophon' which makes no sense except to highlight the absurdities to which censorship leads
58 *Ovid* if he courted out of the *Amores* he would be quite forward
61 *proud stag . . . velvet head* Subtle is wearing a doctor's velvet hat whose texture is like that of the plush on a stag's antlers

But, for your sake, I'd choke, ere I would change
An article of breath, with such a puck-fist—
Come let's be gone.

SUBTLE   Pray you, le' me speak with you.

DAPPER

His worship calls you, Captain.

FACE   I am sorry,   65
I e'er embarked myself, in such a business.

DAPPER

Nay, good sir. He did call you.

FACE   Will he take, then?

SUBTLE

First, hear me—

FACE   Not a syllable, 'less you take.

SUBTLE

Pray ye, sir—

FACE   Upon no terms, but an *assumpsit*

SUBTLE

Your humour must be law.

                              He takes the money

FACE   Why now, sir, talk.   70
Now, I dare hear you with mine honour. Speak.
So may this gentleman too.

SUBTLE   Why, sir—

FACE   No whispering.

SUBTLE

'Fore heaven, you do not apprehend the loss
You do yourself, in this.

FACE   Wherein? For what?

SUBTLE

Marry, to be so importunate for one,   75
That, when he has it, will undo you all:
He'll win up all the money i' the town.

FACE

How!

SUBTLE Yes. And blow up gamester, after gamester,

---

63 *puck-fist* puff-ball (i.e. wind-bag)
69 *assumpsit* legal term; lit. 'he has taken'; a voluntary, oral contract sealed with some form
    of payment
78 *blow up* ruin

As they do crackers, in a puppet-play.
If I do give him a familiar,   80
Give you him all you play for; never set him:
For he will have it.
FACE   You're mistaken, Doctor.
Why, he does ask one but for cups, and horses,
A rifling fly: none o' your great familiars.
DAPPER
Yes, Captain, I would have it, for all games.   85
SUBTLE
I told you so.
FACE   'Slight, that's a new business!
I understood you, a tame bird, to fly
Twice in a term, or so; on Friday nights,
When you had left the office: for a nag,
Of forty, or fifty shillings.
DAPPER   Ay, 'tis true, sir,   90
But I do think, now, I shall leave the law,
And therefore—
FACE   Why, this changes quite the case!
D'you think, that I dare move him?
DAPPER   If you please, sir,
All's one to him, I see.
FACE   What! For that money?
I cannot with my conscience. Nor should you   95
Make the request, methinks.
DAPPER   No, sir, I mean
To add consideration.
FACE   Why, then, sir,
I'll try. Say, that it were for all games, Doctor?
SUBTLE
I say, then, not a mouth shall eat for him
At any ordinary, but o' the score,   100
That is a gaming mouth, conceive me.

79   *crackers* fireworks
81   *set him* lay a wager with him
87   *I understood you* I thought you meant
97   *consideration* payment
99–100 *not a mouth . . . o' the score* because of him no gambler in town will be able to eat unless
       they chalk it up on the slate
100   *ordinary* eating house

[44]

FACE   Indeed!

SUBTLE

He'll draw you all the treasure of the realm,
If it be set him.

FACE   Speak you this from art?

SUBTLE

Ay, sir, and reason too: the ground of art.
He's o' the only best complexion,   105
The Queen of Fairy loves.

FACE   What! Is he!

SUBTLE   Peace.

He'll overhear you. Sir, should she but see him—

FACE

What?

SUBTLE   Do not you tell him.

FACE   Will he win at cards too?

SUBTLE

The spirits of dead Holland, living Isaac,
You'd swear, were in him: such a vigorous luck   110
As cannot be resisted. 'Slight he'll put
Six o' your gallants, to a cloak, indeed.

FACE

A strange success, that some man shall be born to!

SUBTLE

He hears you, man—

DAPPER   Sir, I'll not be ingrateful.

FACE

Faith, I have a confidence in his good nature: 115
You hear, he says, he will not be ingrateful.

SUBTLE

Why, as you please, my venture follows yours.

FACE

Troth, do it, Doctor. Think him trusty, and make him.
He may make us both happy in an hour:
Win some five thousand pound, and send us two on't.   120

---

103 *art* occult knowledge
109 *dead Holland, living Isaac* John and Isaac Holland were the first Dutch alchemists
111–12 *put . . . to a cloak* he'll reduce six gallants to nothing but their cloaks
117 *my venture . . . yours* I'll risk it if you will
119 *happy* rich (the Latin *beatus* translates as both)

DAPPER
Believe it, and I will, sir.
FACE   And you shall, sir.
You have heard all?
DAPPER   No, what was't? Nothing, I sir.
                                        FACE *takes him aside*

FACE
Nothing?
DAPPER   A little, sir.
FACE   Well, a rare star
Reigned, at your birth.
DAPPER   At mine, sir? No.
FACE   The Doctor
Swears that you are—
SUBTLE   Nay, Captain, you'll tell all, now.   125
FACE
Allied to the Queen of Fairy.
DAPPER   Who? That I am?
Believe it, no such matter—
FACE   Yes, and that
Yo' were born with a caul o' your head.
DAPPER   Who says so?
FACE   Come.
You know it well enough, though you dissemble it.
DAPPER
I'fac, I do not. You are mistaken.
FACE   How!   130
Swear by your fac? And in a thing so known
Unto the Doctor? How shall we, sir, trust you
I' the other matter? Can we ever think,
When you have won five, or six thousand pound,
You'll send us shares in't, by this rate?
DAPPER   By Jove, sir,   135
I'll win ten thousand pound, and send you half.
I'fac's no oath.

128   *born with a caul* a sign of good luck
130   *I'fac* in faith
135   *Jove* Gad Q
137   *fac's* fac is Q

SUBTLE   No, no, he did but jest.

FACE

Go to. Go, thank the Doctor, He's your friend
To take it so.

DAPPER   I thank his worship.

FACE   So?

Another angel.

DAPPER   Must I?

FACE   Must you? 'Slight,   140
What else is thanks? Will you be trivial?

                        [*Gives money* to SUBTLE]
                        Doctor,

When must he come, for his familiar?

DAPPER

Shall I not ha' it with me?

SUBTLE   O, good sir!
There must a world of ceremonies pass,
You must be bathed, and fumigated, first;   145
Besides, the Queen of Fairy does not rise,
Till it be noon.

FACE   Not, if she danced, tonight.

SUBTLE

And she must bless it.

FACE   Did you never see
Her royal Grace, yet?

DAPPER   Whom?

FACE   Your aunt of Fairy?

SUBTLE

Not, since she kissed him, in the cradle, Captain,   150
I can resolve you that.

FACE   Well, see her Grace,
Whate'er it cost you, for a thing that I know!
It will be somewhat hard to compass: but,
How ever, see her. You are made, believe it,
If you can see her. Her Grace is a lone woman,   155

138 *He's* He is Q
141 *trivial* petty
147 *tonight* last night
151 *resolve you that* answer that for you
152 *for* on account of

[47]

And very rich, and if she take a fancy,
She will do strange things. See her, at any hand.
'Slid, she may hap to leave you all she has!
It is the Doctor's fear.

DAPPER   How will't be done, then?

FACE

Let me alone, take you no thought. Do you   160
But say to me, Captain, I'll see her Grace.

DAPPER

Captain, I'll see her Grace.

FACE   Enough.   *One knocks without*

SUBTLE   Who's there?

Anon. [*To* FACE] (Conduct him forth, by the back way.)
Sir, against one o'clock, prepare yourself.
Till when you must be fasting; only, take   165
Three drops of vinegar, in, at your nose;
Two at your mouth; and one, at either ear;
Then, bathe your fingers' ends; and wash your eyes;
To sharpen your five senses; and, cry *hum*,
Thrice; and then *buz*, as often; and then, come.   170

FACE

Can you remember this?

DAPPER   I warrant you.

FACE

Well, then, away. 'Tis, but your bestowing
Some twenty nobles, 'mong her Grace's servants;
And, put on a clean shirt: you do not know
What grace her Grace may do you in clean linen.   175

                                        [*Exeunt*]

Act I, Scene iii

                    [*Enter*] SUBTLE

SUBTLE [*To* DRUGGER]

Come in. [*He turns and calls out*]
          (Good wives, I pray you forbear me, now.
Troth I can do you no good, till afternoon.)

---

174   *clean shirt* fairies are traditionally particular about cleanliness

1   *Good wives* this is addressed to some putative clients outside

[*Enter* DRUGGER]

What is your name, say you, Abel Drugger?

DRUGGER   Yes, sir.

SUBTLE

A seller of tobacco?

DRUGGER   Yes, sir.

SUBTLE   'Umh.

Free of the Grocers?

DRUGGER   Ay, and't please you.

SUBTLE   Well—   5

Your business, Abel?

DRUGGER   This, and't please your worship,

I am a young beginner, and am building

Of a new shop, and't like your worship; just,

At corner of a street: (here's the plot on't.)

And I would know, by art, sir, of your worship,   10

Which way I should make my door, by necromancy.

And, where my shelves. And, which should be for boxes.

And, which for pots. I would be glad to thrive, sir.

And, I was wished to your worship, by a gentleman,

One Captain Face, that says you know men's planets,   15

And their good angels, and their bad.

SUBTLE   I do,

If I do see 'em—

[*Enter* FACE]

FACE   What! My honest Abel?

Thou art well met, here!

DRUGGER   Troth, sir, I was speaking,

Just, as your worship came here, of your worship.

I pray you, speak for me to master Doctor.   20

FACE

He shall do anything. Doctor, do you hear?

This is my friend, Abel, an honest fellow,

He lets me have good tobacco, and he does not

---

5 *Free of the grocers* a member of the Grocers' guild or company
9 *plot* groundplan
14 *wished to* recommended

Sophisticate it, with sack-lees, or oil,
Nor washes it in muscadel, and grains,   25
Nor buries it, in gravel, under ground,
Wrapped up in greasy leather, or pissed clouts:
But keeps it in fine lily-pots, that opened,
Smell like conserve of roses, or French beans.
He has his maple block, his silver tongs,   30
Winchester pipes, and fire of juniper.
A neat, spruce-honest-fellow, and no gold-smith.

SUBTLE

He's a fortunate fellow, that I am sure on—

FACE

Already, sir, ha' you found it? Lo' thee Abel!

SUBTLE

And, in right way toward riches—

FACE   Sir.

SUBTLE   This summer,   35
He will be of the clothing of his company:
And, next spring, called to the scarlet. Spend what he can.

FACE

What, and so little beard?

SUBTLE   Sir, you must think,
He may have a receipt, to make hair come.

---

24   *Sophisticate . . . oil* William Barclay records, 'Some . . . haue *Tobacco* from *Florida* indeede, but because either it is exhausted of spiritualitie, or the radicall humor is spent, and wasted, or it hath gotten moysture by the way, or it hath been dried for expedition in the Sunne, or carried too negligently, they sophisticate and farde the same in sundrie sortes with blacke spice, *Galanga, aqua vitae,* Spanish wine, Anise seeds, oyle of Spicke and such like.' *Nepenthes, or the vertues of Tabacco,* Edinburgh, 1614, A4v–A5

25   *muscadel* a fragrant white wine
     grains spice

27   *pissed clouts* rags dampened with urine

30–1   *maple block . . . silver tongs, Winchester pipes . . . fire of juniper* the maple block is for shredding the tobacco leaf; the silver tongs for holding hot coals; Winchester made famously good tobacco pipes; the fire of Juniper wood (very long-burning) enables customers to light their pipes in Abel's shop which, typically, is arranged for the consumption, as well as purchase, of tobacco

32   *gold-smith* usurer

36   *of the clothing of his company* i.e. Drugger will be made a livery-man of his company. Each of the trade guilds and companies had a distinctive livery

37   *called to the scarlet* be made a sherriff

38   *and so little beard?* and so young?

But he'll be wise, preserve his youth, and fine for't: 40
His fortune looks for him, another way.

FACE

'Slid, Doctor, how canst thou know this so soon?
I am amused at that!

SUBTLE   By a rule, Captain,
In metoposcopy, which I do work by,
A certain star i'the forehead, which you see not.   45
Your chestnut, or your olive-coloured face
Does never fail: and your long ear doth promise.
I knew't, by certain spots too, in his teeth,
And on the nail of his mercurial finger.

FACE

Which finger's that?

SUBTLE   His little finger. Look.   50
Y'were born upon a Wednesday?

DRUGGER   Yes, indeed, sir.

SUBTLE

The thumb, in chiromanty, we give Venus;
The forefinger to Jove; the midst, to Saturn;
The ring to Sol; the least, to Mercury:
Who was the lord, sir, of his horoscope,   55
His house of life being Libra, which foreshowed,
He should be a merchant, and should trade with balance.

FACE

Why, this is strange! Is't not, honest Nab?

---

40 *fine for't* H.&S. read this as meaning 'pay the fine for refusing office'; but it may simply
    mean 'and be fine because of it'

43 *amused* amazed; bewildered

44 *metoposcopy* the art of reading character from physiognomy

46–7 *Your chestnut . . . fail* 'The colours of the Body, and especially of the face denote the
    Humour and inclination of the person . . . Those that be chestnut or olive colour are
    Jovialists and honest people, open without painting or cheating', R. Sanders,
    Physionomie and Chiromancie, Metoposcopie, London, 1653, pp. 166–7

49 *mercurial finger* the little finger; each finger is assigned a separate planet in J. B. Porta's
    Coelestis Physiognomoniae, Naples, 1603, lib. v, cap. xiii

52 *chiromanty* palmistry

54–7 *the least . . . balance* Libra is ruled, not by Mercury, but by Venus. But Mercury is a more
    encouraging ruling planet for the aspiring business man. (Jonson's own sign, Gemini, is
    ruled by Mercury)

57 *trade with balance* the scales are the sign of Libra

SUBTLE

    There is a ship now, coming from Ormus,

    That shall yield him, such a commodity   60

    Of drugs—[*looking at plan*]

               this is the west, and this the south?

DRUGGER

    Yes, sir.

SUBTLE And those are your two sides?

DRUGGER   Ay, sir.

SUBTLE

    Make me your door, then, south; your broad side, west:

    And, on the east side of your shop, aloft,

    Write *Mathlai, Tarmiel,* and *Baraborat*;   65

    Upon the north part, *Rael, Velel, Thiel.*

    They are the names of those mercurial spirits,

    That do fright flies from boxes.

DRUGGER   Yes, sir.

SUBTLE   And

    Beneath your threshold, bury me a loadstone

    To draw in gallants, that wear spurs: the rest,   70

    They'll seem to follow.

FACE   That's a secret, Nab!

SUBTLE

    And, on your stall, a puppet, with a vice,

    And a court-fucus, to call city-dames.

    You shall deal much, with minerals.

DRUGGER   Sir, I have,

    At home, already—

SUBTLE   Ay, I know, you have arsenic,   75

    Vitriol, sal-tartar, argaile, alkali,

---

59 *Ormus* Hormuz on the Persian Gulf, source of much spice

65–6 *Mathlai. . . . Thiel* quoted from the *Heptameron, seu Elementa magica Pietri Abano Philosophi* (appended to Cornelius Agrippa's *De Occulta Philosophia* Paris?, no date)

67 *mercurial* Mercurian Q

68 *fright flies from boxes* protect your stores from flies

69 *loadstone* magnet

71 *seem* be seen (a Latinism, *videri*)

72 *vice* wire mechanism for operating the puppet

73 *fucus* cosmetic; one used at court would be desirable to socially-aspiring city women

76 *Vitriol* sulphuric acid

    sal-tartar carbonate of potash

    argaile cream of tartar

    alkali caustic soda

Cinoper: I know all. This fellow, Captain
Will come, in time, to be a great distiller,
And give a say (I will not say directly,
But very fair) at the philosopher's stone.   80
FACE
Why, how now, Abel! Is this true?
DRUGGER   Good Captain,
What must I give?
FACE   Nay, I'll not counsel thee.
Thou hear'st, what wealth (he says, spend what thou canst)
Th'art like to come to.
DRUGGER   I would gi' him a crown.
FACE
A crown! And toward such a fortune? Heart,   85
Thou shalt rather gi' him thy shop. No gold about thee?
DRUGGER
Yes, I have a portague, I ha' kept this half year.
FACE
Out on thee, Nab; 'Slight, there was such an offer—
'Shalt keep't no longer, I'll gi'it him for thee?
Doctor, Nab prays your worship, to drink this:
                          [*Gives money to* SUBTLE]   90
                              and swears
He will appear more grateful, as your skill
Does raise him in the world.
DRUGGER   I would entreat
Another favour of his worship.
FACE   What is't, Nab?
DRUGGER
But, to look over, sir, my almanack,
And cross out my ill days, that I may neither   95
Bargain, nor trust upon them.
FACE   That he shall, Nab.
Leave it, it shall be done, 'gainst afternoon.

77 *Cinoper* red mercuric sulphide
79 *give a say* make a try for
87 *portague* a Portuguese gold coin
95 *ill days* days that are astrologically inauspicious
97 *'gainst* by

SUBTLE
And a direction for his shelves.
FACE   Now, Nab?
Art thou well pleased, Nab?
DRUGGER   Thank, sir, both your worships.
FACE   Away.
                   [*Exit* DRUGGER]
Why, now, you smoky persecutor of nature!   100
Now, do you see, that something's to be done,
Beside your beech-coal, and your corsive waters,
Your crosslets, crucibles, and cucurbites?
You must have stuff, brought home to you, to work on?
And, yet, you think, I am at no expense,   105
In searching out these veins, then following 'em,
Then trying 'em out. 'Fore God, my intelligence
Costs me more money, than my share oft comes to,
In these rare works.
SUBTLE   You are pleasant, sir.

          [*Enter*] DOL

                How now?

Act I, Scene iv

FACE
What says, my dainty Dolkin?
DOL   Yonder fish-wife
Will not away. And there's your giantess,
The bawd of Lambeth.
SUBTLE   Heart, I cannot speak with 'em.
DOL
Not, afore night, I have told 'em, in a voice,
Thorough the trunk, like one of your familiars.   5

---

102 *beech-coal* beech wood made the best charcoal
      corsive corrosive
103 *crosslets* melting pots
      cucurbites gourd-shaped retorts used in distillation
107 *intelligence* information

  3 *Lambeth* noted for prostitutes and thieves
  5 *Thorough the trunk* i.e. through a speaking tube

But I have spied Sir Epicure Mammon—
SUBTLE   Where?
DOL
    Coming along, at the far end of the lane,
    Slow of his feet, but earnest of his tongue,
    To one, that's with him.
SUBTLE   Face, go you, and shift.   [*Exit* FACE]
    Dol, you must presently make ready too—   10
DOL
    Why, what's the matter?
SUBTLE   O, I did look for him
    With the sun's rising: marvel, he could sleep!
    This is the day, I am to perfect for him
    The *magisterium*, our great work, the stone;
    And yield it, made, into his hands: of which,   15
    He has, this month, talked, as he were possessed.
    And, now, he's dealing pieces on't, away.
    Methinks, I see him, entering ordinaries,
    Dispensing for the pox; and plaguey-houses,
    Reaching his dose; walking Moorfields for lepers;   20
    And offering citizens' wives pomander-bracelets,
    As his preservative, made of the elixir;
    Searching the spittle, to make old bawds young;
    And the highways, for beggars, to make rich:
    I see no end of his labours. He will make   25
    Nature ashamed of her long sleep: when art,
    Who's but a step-dame, shall do more, than she,
    In her best love to mankind, ever could.
    If his dream last, he'll turn the age, to gold.   [*Exeunt*]

---

   9 *shift* change
 14 *magisterium* master work
 16 *possessed* possess'd on't Q
 17 *dealing . . . away* giving parts of it away (in imagination)
 20 *Reaching* offering
     Moorfields a stretch of reclaimed marshland which in Jonson's time was being laid out
     in parks. It was noted for beggars, and lepers were allowed to beg there
 21 *pomander-bracelets* a pomander was a perfumed ball carried as a protection against
     infection (and smells)
 23 *spittle* hospital
 27 *step-dame* the debate as to the respective roles of Art and Nature was a commonplace.
     See, e.g., *The Winter's Tale*, IV. iv.79–102

Act II, Scene i

[*Enter*] MAMMON, SURLY

MAMMON

Come on, sir. Now, you set your foot on shore
In *novo orbe*; here's the rich Peru:
And there within, sir, are the golden mines,
Great Solomon's Ophir! He was sailing to't,
Three years, but we have reached it in ten months.   5
This is the day, wherein, to all my friends,
I will pronounce the happy word, be rich.
This day, you shall be *spectatissimi*.
You shall no more deal with the hollow die,
Or the frail card. No more be at charge of keeping   10
The livery-punk, for the young heir, that must
Seal, at all hours, in his shirt. No more
If he deny, ha' him beaten to't, as he is
That brings him the commodity. No more
Shall thirst of satin, or the covetous hunger   15
Of velvet entrails, for a rude-spun cloak,

1–5 *Now, you set your foot . . . ten months* Mammon is promising Surly a 'new world' of wealth.
     The discovery of the Americas by Renaissance voyagers became a potent metaphor for much
     non-topographical experience of the time. Solomon was believed to have possessed the
     Philosopher's Stone and to have fetched his wealth 'once in three years' from Ophir (*I Kings* x.22)
  2 *novo orbe* the new world; i.e. America; both a metaphor for wealth and its source (through
     imports)
     Peru synonym for great wealth; the location of El Dorado
  8 *spectatissimi* (Lat.) very much regarded
  9 *hollow die* loaded dice (hollowed and then weighted with lead)
10–14 *No more . . . commodity* an allusion to the 'commodity swindle' (described in Greene's
     Defence of Coney-Catching, The Works of Robert Greene, ed. A. B. Grosart, London 1881–6,
     vol. xi, p. 53) by which a borrower was constrained to take all or part of a loan in the form
     of often unsaleable goods (see III.iv.87–99). The 'livery-punk' is a prostitute ('livery' implies
     that she is part of the regular retinue) who, by compromising the young heir in *déshabille*,
     furthers the money-lender's attempts to make him 'seal' such an unprofitable bargain
 11 *the young* my yong Q
 16 *velvet entrails* velvet linings. The contemporary fashion for 'slashing' the top layer of fabric
     to allow the contrasting inner stuff to show through could be disturbingly
     reminiscent of gaping wounds. See Lovelace's 'La Bella Bona Roba' 'whose white-sattin
     upper coat of skin/[Is] Cut upon velvet rich incarnadin'

To be displayed at Madam Augusta's, make
The sons of sword, and hazard fall before
The golden calf, and on their knees, whole nights,
Commit idolatory with wine, and trumpets: 20
Or go a-feasting, after drum and ensign.
No more of this. You shall start up young viceroys,
And have your punks, and punketees, my Surly.
And unto thee, I speak it first, be rich.
Where is my Subtle there? Within ho?

FACE *Within*   Sir. 25
He'll come to you, by and by.

MAMMON   That's his fire-drake,
His lungs, his Zephyrus, he that puffs his coals,
Till he firk nature up, in her own centre.
You are not faithful, sir. This night, I'll change
All, that is metal, in thy house, to gold. 30
And, early in the morning, will I send
To all the plumbers, and the pewterers,
And buy their tin, and lead up: and to Lothbury,
For all the copper.

SURLY   What, and turn that too?

MAMMON
Yes, and I'll purchase Devonshire, and Cornwall, 35
And make them perfect Indies! You admire now?

17 *Madam Augusta* presumably a brothel madam
18 *The sons of sword, and hazard* thugs and gamblers
19 *golden calf* a false idol (*Exodus* xxxii)
22 *start up* generate
23 *punketees* little whores
26 *fire-drake* firey dragon or meteor; here used figuratively for fire-maker
27 *lungs* bellows; i.e. assistant
   Zephyrus the west wind personified
28 *firk* stir
29 *faithful* trusting
30 *thy* my Q (the F reading may be an error)
33 *Lothbury* 'This streete is possessed for the most part by Founders, that cast Candlestickes, Chafingdishes, Spice mortars and such like Copper or Laton workes.' John Stow, *A Survey of London,* ed. C. L. Kingsford, Oxford, 1908, p. 277
35 *Devonshire, and Cornwall* the site of tin and copper mines
36 *perfect Indies* the West Indies, thought to be rich in 'spice and mine' (Donne, 'The Sun Rising')
   admire are struck

SURLY

  No faith.

MAMMON But when you see th'effects of the great med'cine!

  Of which one part projected on a hundred

  Of Mercury, or Venus, or the Moon,

  Shall turn it, to as many of the Sun;   40

  Nay, to a thousand, so *ad infinitum*:

  You will believe me.

SURLY   Yes, when I see't, I will.

  But, if my eyes do cozen me so (and I

  Giving 'em no occasion) sure, I'll have

  A whore, shall piss 'em out, next day.

MAMMON   Ha! Why?   45

  Do you think, I fable with you? I assure you,

  He that has once the flower of the sun,

  The perfect ruby, which we call elixir,

  Not only can do that, but by its virtue,

  Can confer honour, love, respect, long life,   50

  Give safety, valour: yea, and victory,

  To whom he will. In eight, and twenty days,

  I'll make an old man, of fourscore, a child.

SURLY

  No doubt, he's that already.

MAMMON   Nay, I mean,

  Restore his years, renew him, like an eagle,   55

  To the fifth age; make him get sons, and daughters,

  Young giants; as our philosophers have done

  (The ancient patriarchs afore the flood)

  But taking, once a week, on a knife's point,

  The quantity of a grain of mustard, of it: 60

  Become stout Marses, and beget young Cupids.

39–40 *Mercury . . . the sun* Mercury is quicksilver; Venus stands for copper, the moon for silver
    and the sun for gold

47–8 *flower of the sun . . . perfect ruby . . . elixir* all synonyms for the Philosopher's Stone

  55 *like an eagle* 'Thy youth is renewed like the eagle's', *Psalms* ciii.5

  56 *the fifth age* 'The *fifth* age, named *Mature Manhood,* hath . . . fifteen yeares of continuance,
    and therefore makes his progress so far as six and fifty yeares' (quoted from *The Treasury
    of Ancient and Modern Times,* 1613, by Malone on *As You Like It,* II.vii.151)

  58 *ancient patriarchs* the longevity of the Patriarchs was attributed to their knowledge of
    alchemy

SURLY

    The decayed Vestals of Pict-Hatch would thank you,

    That keep the fire alive, there.

MAMMON   'Tis the secret

    Of nature, naturized 'gainst all infections,

    Cures all diseases, coming of all causes,   65

    A month's grief, in a day; a year's, in twelve:

    And, of what age soever, in a month.

    Past all the doses, of your drugging Doctors.

    I'll undertake, withal, to fright the plague

    Out o' the kingdom, in three months.

SURLY   And I'll   70

    Be bound, the players shall sing your praises, then,

    Without their poets.

MAMMON   Sir, I'll do't. Meantime,

    I'll give away so much, unto my man,

    Shall serve th' whole city, with preservative,

    Weekly, each house his dose, and at the rate—   75

SURLY

    As he that built the waterwork, does with water?

MAMMON

    You are incredulous.

SURLY   Faith, I have a humour,

    I would not willingly be gulled. Your stone

    Cannot transmute me.

MAMMON   Pertinax, Surly,

    Will you believe antiquity? Records?   80

    I'll show you a book, where Moses, and his sister,

---

62 *The decayed Vestals of Pict-Hatch* Pict-Hatch (just south of where Goswell Road and Old
     Street now meet) was a haunt of prostitutes. Vestals were traditionally virgin temple
     servers. The fire maintained by these vestals is presumably that of venereal infection

64 *nature, naturized* scholastic philosophy distinguished between creating nature (*natura
     naturans*) and created nature (*natura naturata*). The stone is part of creat*ed* nature

71–2 *the players . . . poets* the London theatres were closed while the plague was rife because
     they were thought to be places of infection and also to invite infection as retribution for
     the immorality they housed. The players would sing Mammon's praises if they found
     themselves in work again

76 *the waterwork* probably the pump-house built by Bevis Bulmer at Broken Wharf in 1594.
     This supplied Cheapside and Fleet Street with water from the Thames

77 *I have a humour* it is my temperament

81–3 *Moses . . . Adam* Mammon is not alone in his attribution of alchemical lore to Moses,
     Solomon and Adam. See *H.&S.* for references

And Solomon have written, of the art;
Ay, and a treatise penned by Adam.

SURLY   How!

MAMMON

O' the philosopher's stone, and in High Dutch.

SURLY

Did Adam write, sir, in High Dutch?

MAMMON   He did: 85
Which proves it was the primitive tongue.

SURLY   What paper?

MAMMON

On cedar board.

SURLY   O that, indeed (they say)
Will last 'gainst worms.

MAMMON   'Tis like your Irish wood,
'Gainst cobwebs. I have a piece of Jason's fleece, too,
Which was no other, than a book of alchemy,   90
Writ in large sheepskin, a good fat ram-vellum.
Such was Pythagoras' thigh, Pandora's tub;
And, all that fable of Medea's charms,
The manner of our work: the bulls, our furnace,
Still breathing fire; our *argent-vive*, the dragon;   95
The dragon's teeth, mercury sublimate,
That keeps the whiteness, hardness, and the biting;
And they are gathered, into Jason's helm,
(Th' alembic) and then sowed in Mars his field,

84 *High Dutch* hoch Deutsch (high German); Joannes Goropius Becanus, a Flemish physician,
    claimed that German was the original language and that the early Germans were not at
    the Tower of Babel. He declared this in a treatise called *Hermathena* (c. 1580)

87–9 *cedar board . . . Irish wood* cedar wood was known for its durability, Irish wood for its
    ability to repel spiders and insects

89 *Jason's fleece* 'Cornelius Agrippa maketh mention of some Philosophers that held the
    skinne of the sheepe that bare the golden fleece, to be nothing but a booke of Alcumy
    written vpon it' *The Works of Thomas Nashe*, ed. R. B. McKerrow, Oxford, 1966, iii, 221

92 *Pythagoras' thigh* supposedly golden (*Diogenes Laertius*, viii.i). Martin Delrio associates
    both this and Pandora's box (*tub*) with alchemy in his *Disquisitiones Magicae*, 1599

93–100 *that fable . . .are fixed* in order to gain the golden fleece Jason had to yoke and plough
    with two brazen-footed, fire-breathing bulls. He then had to sow dragons' teeth which
    sprang up as armed warriors. Medea, his witch-lover, taught him how to cope

95 *argent-vive* quicksilver

96 *mercury sublimate* chloride of mercury – a corrosive (hence the 'biting')

99 *alembic* distilling apparatus
    Mars his field an old genitive form (= Mars' field) Mars stands for iron

And, thence, sublimed so often, till they are fixed.   100
Both this, th' Hesperian garden, Cadmus' story,
Jove's shower, the boon of Midas, Argus' eyes,
Boccace his Demogorgon, thousands more,
All abstract riddles of our stone. How now?

Act II, Scene ii

[*Enter*] FACE [*dressed as bellows-man to them*]

MAMMON
Do we succeed? Is our day come? And holds it?
FACE
The evening will set red, upon you, sir;
You have colour for it, crimson: the red ferment
Has done his office. Three hours hence, prepare you
To see projection.
MAMMON   Pertinax, my Surly,   5
Again, I say to thee, aloud: be rich.
This day, thou shalt have ingots: and, tomorrow,
Give lords th'affront. Is it, my Zephyrus, right?
Blushes the bolt's head?
FACE   Like a wench with child, sir,
That were, but now, discovered to her master.   10
MAMMON
Excellent witty Lungs! My only care is,
Where to get stuff, enough now, to project on,

---

101 *th' Hesperian garden* site of golden apples guarded by a dragon
101 *Cadmus' story* Cadmus founded Thebes on the spot where he killed a dragon, then planted
     its teeth which sprang up as warriors. All but five of these warriors killed each other
102 *Jove's shower* Jove entered Danae as a shower of gold
     the boon of Midas Bacchus gave Midas the dubious gift of turning all he touched to gold
     Argus' eyes Argus was a dog with a hundred eyes whom Juno set to guard the woman-
     heifer Io whom her husband, Jupiter, loved
103 *Boccace his Demogorgon* a primeval god named by Boccaccio in his *Genealogica Deorum*.
     Demogorgon is also mentioned by Milton and Spenser
104 *abstract riddles* allegories

3 *red ferment* 'Red is last in the work of *Alkimy*', Norton, *Ordinal*, in *T.C.B.*,p. 56; 'ferment'
   is leaven
8 *Give lords th'affront* look lords in the eye as their equal
9 *bolt's head* 'a globular flask with a long cylindrical neck' (*OED*); it 'blushes' as it reddens

This town will not half serve me.

FACE   No, sir? Buy

The covering off o' churches.

MAMMON   That's true.

FACE   Yes.

Let 'em stand bare, as do their auditory.   15

Or cap 'em, new, with shingles.

MAMMON   No, good thatch:

Thatch will lie light upo' the rafters, Lungs.

Lungs, I will manumit thee, from the furnace;

I will restore thee thy complexion, Puff,

Lost in the embers; and repair this brain,   20

Hurt wi' the fume o' the metals.

FACE   I have blown, sir,

Hard, for your worship; thrown by many a coal,

When 'twas not beech; weighed those I put in, just,

To keep your heat still even; these bleared eyes

Have waked, to read your several colours, sir,   25

Of the pale citron, the green lion, the crow,

The peacock's tail, the plumed swan.

MAMMON   And, lastly,

Thou hast descried the flower, the *sanguis agni?*

FACE

Yes, sir.

MAMMON Where's master?

FACE   At's prayers, sir, he,

Good man, he's doing his devotions,   30

For the success.

---

13 *Buy* Take Q

15 *auditory* congregation (who remove their hats)

16 *shingles* slats of wood used like roof tiles

18 *manumit* release

23 *when 'twas not beech* in Lyly's *Gallathea* the alchemist says 'I may have onely Beechen coales' II.ii.78

26–7 *pale citron . . . swan* each of these items names a colour and stage in the alchemical process: 'Pale, and Black, wyth falce Cityne, unparfyt Whyte & Red, Pekoks fethers in color gay, the Raynbow whych shall overgoe/The Spottyd Panther wyth the Lyon greene, the Crowys byll bloe as lede;/These shall appere before the parfyt Whyte', Ripley, *Compound of Alchymie,* in *T.C.B.,* p. 88

28 *sanguis agni* 'blood of the lamb' (Lat.); a red indicating successful projection. The term has Christian, sacrificial connotations

MAMMON   Lungs, I will set a period,
To all thy labours: thou shalt be the master
Of my seraglio.
FACE   Good, sir.
MAMMON   But do you hear?
I'll geld you, Lungs.
FACE   Yes, sir.
MAMMON   For I do mean
To have a list of wives, and concubines,   35
Equal with Solomon; who had the stone
Alike, with me: and I will make me, a back
With the elixir, that shall be as tough
As Hercules, to encounter fifty a night.
Th'art sure, thou saw'st it blood?
FACE   Both blood, and spirit, sir.   40
MAMMON
I will have all my beds, blown up; not stuffed:
Down is too hard. And then, mine oval room,
Filled with such pictures, as Tiberius took
From Elephantis: and dull Aretine
But coldly imitated. Then, my glasses,   45
Cut in more subtle angles, to disperse,
And multiply the figures, as I walk
Naked between my *succubae*. My mists
I'll have of perfume, vapoured 'bout the room,
To lose ourselves in; and my baths, like pits   50
To fall into: from whence, we will come forth,
And roll us dry in gossamer, and roses.
(Is it arrived at ruby?) – Where I spy
A wealthy citizen, or rich lawyer,
Have a sublimed pure wife, unto that fellow   55
I'll send a thousand pound, to be my cuckold.
FACE
And I shall carry it?

33 *seraglio* harem; seraglia Q, F
41 *beds, blown up* Lampridius, *Elagabalus,* xxv
43–4 Suetonius, *Tiberius,* cap. xliii
44 *Aretine* Pietro Aretino (1492–1550); Italian poet whose *Sonnetti Lussuriosi* (1523) illustrated
     by Giulio Romano were notorious erotica of their time
45 *glasses* Seneca, *Naturales Quaestiones,* I.xvi, refers to Hostius Quadra's use of mirrors to
     arouse himself
48 *succubae* demons assuming female form in order to have sexual intercourse with humans

MAMMON   No. I'll ha' no bawds,
But fathers, and mothers. They will do it best.
Best of all others. And, my flatterers
Shall be the pure, and gravest of Divines,   60
That I can get for money. My mere fools,
Eloquent burgesses, and then my poets,
The same that writ so subtly of the fart,
Whom I will entertain, still, for that subject.
The few, that would give out themselves, to be   65
Court, and town stallions, and, eachwhere, belie
Ladies, who are known most innocent, for them;
Those will I beg, to make me eunuchs of:
And they shall fan me with ten ostrich tails
Apiece, made in a plume, to gather wind.   70
We will be brave, Puff, now we ha' the med'cine.
My meat, shall all come in, in Indian shells,
Dishes of agate, set in gold, and studded,
With emeralds, sapphires, hyacinths, and rubies.
The tongues of carps, dormice, and camels' heels,   75
Boiled i' the spirit of Sol, and dissolved pearl,
(Apicius' diet, 'gainst the epilepsy)
And I will eat these broths, with spoons of amber,
Headed with diamant, and carbuncle.
My footboy shall eat pheasants, calvered salmons,   80
Knots, godwits, lampreys: I myself will have

---

58   *They will . . . all others* not in Q
60   *the pure, and gravest* purest and gravest
       pure best Q
62   *burgesses* members of Parliament
63   *that writ . . .of the fan* perhaps the anonymous author of 'The fart Censured in the
       Parliament House' – a ballad commemorating an event in 1607. But Jonson himself wrote
       much of farts in 'The Famous Voyage'
74   *hyacinths* not the flowers but precious blue stones
75   *tongues of carps* 'The tongues of *Carps* are noted to be chioce and costly meat', Isaac
       Walton, *The Compleat Angler* (1653), Oxford, 1935, p. 149
       dormice the Romans ate them (Apicius gives a recipe), and the practice has lately been
       revived in England by a firm hoping to catch the novelty delicacy market *camels' heels*
       Lampridius, *Elagabalus*, xx, tells how this emperor ate these 'in imitation of Apicius'—
       he also ate the beards of mullets
77   *Apicius* the Roman author of *Artis Magiricae* (The Art of Cooking)
80   *calvered* a culinary process only applicable to fresh firm fish
81   *Knots* a species of snipe
       godwits marsh birds, similar to curlews
       lampreys eel-shaped fish

The beards of barbels, served, instead of salads;
Oiled mushrooms; and the swelling unctuous paps
Of a fat pregnant sow, newly cut off,
Dressed with an exquisite, and poignant sauce;   85
For which, I'll say unto my cook, there's gold,
Go forth, and be a knight.

FACE   Sir, I'll go look
A little, how it heightens.

MAMMON   Do.   [*Exit* FACE]
                        My shirts
I'll have of taffeta-sarsnet, soft, and light
As cobwebs; and for all my other raiment   90
It shall be such, as might provoke the Persian;
Were he to teach the world riot, anew.
My gloves of fishes', and birds' skins, perfumed
With gums of paradise, and eastern air—

SURLY
And do you think to have the stone, with this?   95

MAMMON
No, I do think, t' have all this, with the stone.

SURLY
Why, I have heard, he must be *homo frugi*,
A pious, holy, and religious man,
One free from mortal sin, a very virgin.

MAMMON
That makes it, sir, he is so. But I buy it.   100
My venture brings it me. He, honest wretch,
A notable, superstitious, good soul,
Has worn his knees bare, and his slippers bald,
With prayer, and fasting for it: and, sir, let him
Do it alone, for me, still. Here he comes,   105
Not a profane word, afore him: 'tis poison.

---

82 *barbels* a species of carp with fleshy filaments hanging from its mouth. See note to
    line 75

85 *poignant* piquant

89 *taffeta-sarsnet* a fine soft silk

91 *the Persian* Sardanapalus, king of Ninevah 9 B.C. – of legendary luxury

94 *gums of paradise* incense from the middle East (where the Garden of Eden had supposedly
    been)

97–9 *homo frugi . . . virgin* piety, purity and a lack of material ambition are prerequisite to
      alchemical success

Act II, Scene iii

[Enter] SUBTLE *[to them]*

MAMMON
 Good morrow, Father.
SUBTLE   Gentle son, good morrow,
 And, to your friend, there. What is he, is with you?
MAMMON
 An heretic, that I did bring along,
 In hope, sir, to convert him.
SUBTLE   Son, I doubt
 You're covetous, that thus you meet your time   5
 I' the just point: prevent your day, at morning.
 This argues something, worthy of a fear
 Of importune, and carnal appetite.
 Take heed, you do not cause the blessing leave you,
 With your ungoverned haste. I should be sorry,   10
 To see my labours, now, e'en at perfection,
 Got by long watching, and large patience,
 Not prosper, where my love, and zeal hath placed 'em.
 Which (heaven I call to witness, with yourself,
 To whom, I have poured my thoughts) in all my ends,   15
 Have looked no way, but unto public good,
 To pious uses, and dear charity,
 Now grown a prodigy with men. Wherein
 If you, my son, should now prevaricate,
 And, to your own particular lusts, employ   20
 So great, and catholic a bliss: be sure,
 A curse will follow, yea, and overtake
 Your subtle, and most secret ways.
MAMMON   I know, sir,
 You shall not need to fear me. I but come,

---

 4 *doubt* fear
 6 *I' the just point* punctually, on the dot
    prevent anticipate
 12 *watching* waking
 18 *Now* No Q, F
 19 *prevaricate* walk crookedly (Lat. *praevaricari*)
 21 *catholic* general (as opposed to 'particular', line 20)

To ha' you confute this gentleman.

SURLY   Who is,   25
Indeed, sir, somewhat costive of belief
Toward your stone: would not be gulled.

SUBTLE   Well, son,
All that I can convince him in, is this,
The work is done: bright Sol is in his robe.
We have a med'cine of the triple soul,   30
The glorified spirit. Thanks be to heaven,
And make us worthy of it. Ulen Spiegel.

FACE [*within*]
                    Anon, sir.

                    [*Enter* FACE]

SUBTLE   Look well to the register,
And let your heat, still, lessen by degrees,
To the aludels.

FACE   Yes, sir.   35

SUBTLE   Did you look
O' the bolt's head yet?

FACE   Which, on D, sir?

SUBTLE   Ay.
What's the complexion?

FACE   Whitish.

25 SURLY SVB. Q

29 *bright Sol is in his robe* Sol (the sun), the planet governing gold, is ready to officiate

30 *triple soul* according to scholastic thought there are three kinds of soul: the vegetable
(capable of growth), the animal (capable of reproduction) and the intellectual (capable of
thought). Humans are possessed of all three and are linked to the angels by their intellectual
souls

32 *Ulen Spiegel* lit. 'Owl-glass'; Til Eulen Spiegel is the hero of several German jest books.
He is a practical joker. William Copeland's *Howle glass* was published in England between
1548 and 1560

33 *register* a contrivance – usually consisting of moveable metal plates – for regulating the
passage of air, heat and smoke

35 *aludels* pear-shaped vessels, open at either end; used for sublimation

36 *on D* Face gives the impression of a number of different operations going on concurrently,
each distinguished by a letter of the alphabet

37 *complexion* colour

SUBTLE   Infuse vinegar,
  To draw his volatile substance, and his tincture:
  And let the water in glass E be filtered,
  And put into the gripe's egg. Lute him well;   40
  And leave him closed in *balneo*.
FACE   I will, sir.   [*Exit* FACE]
SURLY
  What a brave language here is? Next to canting?
SUBTLE
  I have another work; you never saw, son,
  That, three days since, passed the philosopher's wheel,
  In the lent heat of Athanor; and's become   45
  Sulphur o' nature.
MAMMON   But 'tis for me?
SUBTLE   What need you?
  You have enough in that is perfect.
MAMMON   O, but—
SUBTLE
  Why, this is covetise!
MAMMON   No, I assure you,
  I shall employ it all, in pious uses,
  Founding of colleges, and grammar schools,   50
  Marrying young virgins, building hospitals,
  And now, and then, a church.

[*Enter* FACE]

SUBTLE   How now?
FACE   Sir, please you,
  Shall I not change the filter?

38, 40 *his . . . him* the use of the personal pronoun is in keeping with the alchemists' belief that
     all matter is animate
  40 *gripe's egg* an egg-shaped pot (a 'gripe' is a vulture)
     Lute stop up the gaps with lute (clay)
  41 *in balneo* in a bath (of boiling water or hot sand)
  42 *canting* cant was the private (though much publicised) language of thieves
  44 *philosopher's wheel* alchemical cycle
  45 *lent* slow (Lat.)
     Athanor a 'digesting furnace' maintaining a low, constant heat
  46 *Sulphur o' nature* pure sulphur in an immutable state

SUBTLE   Marry, yes.
And bring me the complexion of glass B.   [*Exit* FACE]
MAMMON
Ha' you another?
SUBTLE   Yes, son, were I assured   55
Your piety were firm, we would not want
The means to glorify it. But I hope the best:
I mean to tinct C in sand-heat, tomorrow,
And give him imbibition.
MAMMON   Of white oil?
SUBTLE
No, sir, of red. F is come over the helm too,   60
I thank my Maker, in S. Mary's bath,
And shows *lac virginis*. Blessed be heaven.
I sent you of his faeces there, calcined.
Out of that calx, I ha' won the salt of mercury.
MAMMON
By pouring on your rectified water?   65
SUBTLE
Yes, and reverberating in Athanor.

                    [*Enter* FACE]

How now? What colour says it?
FACE   The ground black, sir.
MAMMON
That's your crow's head?
SURLY   Your cockscomb's, is't not?

58 *sand-heat* i.e. in a sand bath
59 *imbibition* steeping in liquid
59–60 *white . . .red* mercury is 'white', sulphur 'red'; the oils would be derivatives of these
61 *S. Mary's bath* the 'bain Marie' of modern cooking
62 *lac virginis* 'Mercurial Water, the Dragon's Tail: it washes and coagulates without any
    manual labour' Ruland, *A Lexicon of Alchemy*, Frankfurt, 1612
63 *faeces* sediment
    calcined reduced to a powder having had its humidity drawn out by heat
64 *calx* the powdery result of calcining
    salt oxide
65 *rectified* distilled
66 *reverberating* being heated by reflected heat
68 *crow's head* blackness resulting from calcination

SUBTLE
   No, 'tis not perfect, would it were the crow.
   That work wants something.
SURLY   (O, I looked for this.   70
   The hay is a-pitching.)
SUBTLE   Are you sure, you loosed 'em
   I' their own menstrue?
FACE   Yes, sir, and then married 'em,
   And put 'em in a bolt's head, nipped to digestion,
   According as you bade me; when I set
   The liquor of Mars to circulation,   75
   In the same heat.
SUBTLE   The process, then, was right.
FACE
   Yes, by the token, sir, the retort broke,
   And what was saved, was put into the pelican,
   And signed with Hermes' seal.
SUBTLE   I think 'twas so.
   We should have a new amalgama.
SURLY   (O, this ferret   80
   Is rank as any pole-cat.)
SUBTLE   But I care not.
   Let him e'en die; we have enough beside,
   In embrion. H has his white shirt on?
FACE   Yes, sir,
   He's ripe for inceration: he stands warm,
   In his ash-fire. I would not, you should let   85

---

71   *The hay is a-pitching* a 'hay' is a net 'pitched' or set in front of rabbits' burrows.
     The metaphor is from the language of coney-catching
71–2 *loosed . . . menstrue* dissolved them in the fluid distilled from them
73   *nipped* sealed
     digestion slow extraction of soluble substances through 'cooking' in a digesting oven
75   *liquor of Mars* molten iron
78   *pelican* an alembic with a tubular head and two curved spouts, each of which re-enter
     the vessel (like a pelican wounding its own breast)
79   *signed with Hermes' seal* hermetically sealed
80   *amalgama* mixture of metals with mercury
80–1 *ferret . . . pole-cat* the images sustain the coney-catching metaphor; pole-cats are smellier
     than ferrets
83   *in embrion* in their early stages
83   *has his white shirt on* has turned white
84   *inceration* bringing the substances to the consistency of soft wax

　　Any die now, if I might counsel, sir,
　　For luck's sake to the rest. It is not good.
MAMMON
　　He says right.
SURLY　　　　　(Ay, are you bolted?)
FACE　　　　　　　　　　　Nay, I know't, sir,
　　I have seen th' ill fortune. What is some three ounces
　　Of fresh materials?
MAMMON　　　　　Is't no more?
FACE　　　　　　　　　　No more, sir,　　　　　　　90
　　Of gold, t'amalgam, with some six of mercury.
MAMMON
　　Away, here's money. What will serve?
FACE　　　　　　　　　　Ask him, sir.
MAMMON
　　How much?
SURLY　　　　Give him nine pound: you may gi' him ten.
SURLY
　　Yes, twenty, and be cozened, do.
MAMMON　　　　　　　There 'tis.
SUBTLE
　　This needs not. But that you will have it, so,　　　95
　　To see conclusions of all. For two
　　Of our inferior works, are at fixation.
　　A third is in ascension. Go your ways.
　　Ha' you set the oil of Luna in kemia?
FACE
　　Yes, sir.
SUBTLE　　And the philosopher's vinegar?
FACE　　　　　　　　　　Ay.　　　　　　[*Exit* FACE]　　100
SURLY
　　We shall have a salad.
MAMMON　　　　　　When do you make projection?
SUBTLE
　　Son, be not hasty. I exalt our med'cine,

88　*bolted* entered the snare (another coney-catching image)
97　*fixation* the process of reducing a volatile substance to a stable form
99　*oil of Luna* white elixir
　　kemia from the Greek χυμξια: alchemy; here it probably implies entrance into the whole process
100　*philosopher's vinegar* either mercury or a corrosive vinegar made of mead
101　*salad* a salad dressing from the oil and vinegar; the term was actually used by alchemists

By hanging him in *balneo vaporoso;*
And giving him solution; then congeal him;
And then dissolve him; then again congeal him;   105
For look, how oft I iterate the work,
So many times, I add unto his virtue.
As, if at first, one ounce convert a hundred,
After his second loose, he'll turn a thousand;
His third solution, ten; his fourth, a hundred.   110
After his fifth, a thousand thousand ounces
Of any imperfect metal, into pure
Silver, or gold, in all examinations,
As good, as any of the natural mine.
Get you your stuff here, against afternoon,   115
Your brass, your pewter, and your andirons.

MAMMON
Not those of iron?

SUBTLE   Yes, you may bring them, too.
We'll change all metals.

SURLY   I believe you, in that.

MAMMON
Then I may send my spits?

SUBTLE   Yes, and your racks.

SURLY
And dripping pans, and pot-hangers, and hooks?   120
Shall he not?

SUBTLE   If he please.

SURLY   To be an ass.

SUBTLE
How, sir!

MAMMON This gent'man, you must bear withal.
I told you, he had no faith.

SURLY   And little hope, sir,
But, much less charity, should I gull my self.

---

103 *balneo vaporoso* a contrivance for suspending vessels in steam
106–7 *how oft . . . virtue* the potency of the stone is increased each time I subject it to the process
        of dissolution and congelation
108 *convert* turn into
109 *loose* dissolution
116 *andirons* metal supports for logs in a fire; fire-dogs
123–4 *faith . . . hope . . . charity* the Cardinal Virtues and all necessary to alchemical success

SUBTLE
  Why, what have you observed, sir, in our art,   125
  Seems so impossible?
SURLY   But your whole work, no more.
  That you should hatch gold in a furnace, sir,
  As they do eggs, in Egypt!
SUBTLE   Sir, do you
  Believe that eggs are hatched so?
SURLY   If I should?
SUBTLE
  Why, I think that the greater miracle.   130
  No egg, but differs from a chicken, more,
  Than metals in themselves.
SURLY   That cannot be.
  The egg's ordained by nature, to that end:
  And is a chicken in *potentia*.
SUBTLE
  The same we say of lead, and other metals,   135
  Which would be gold, if they had time.
MAMMON   And that
  Our art doth further.
SUBTLE   Ay, for 'twere absurd
  To think that nature, in the earth, bred gold
  Perfect, i' the instant. Something went before.
  There must be remote matter.
SURLY   Ay, what is that?   140
SUBTLE
  Marry, we say—
MAMMON   Ay, now it heats: stand Father.
  Pound him to dust—
SUBTLE   It is, of the one part,
  A humid exhalation, which we call
  Materia liquida, or the unctuous water;
  On th' other part, a certain crass, and viscous   145
  Portion of earth; both which, concorporate,

128   *eggs, in Egypt* Pliny mentions eggs hatching on dung-hills in Egypt (*Nat. Hist.*, x.lxxv.153)
131–76 *No egg . . . metals* Subtle's argument is taken, in places almost verbatim, from Martin
    Delrio's *Disquisitiones Magicae*, 1599
140   *remote matter* the first matter
144   *unctuous* oily
145   *crass* dense
146   *concorporate* fused into a single body

Do make the elementary matter of gold:
Which is not, yet, *propria materia*,
But common to all metals, and all stones.
For, where it is forsaken of that moisture   150
And hath more dryness, it becomes a stone;
Where it retains more of the humid fatness,
It turns to sulphur, or to quicksilver:
Who are the parents of all other metals.
Nor can this remote matter, suddenly,   155
Progress so from extreme, unto extreme,
As to grow gold, and leap o'er all the means.
Nature doth, first, beget th' imperfect; then
Proceeds she to the perfect. Of that airy,
And oily water, mercury is engendered;   160
Sulphur o' the fat, and earthy part: the one
(Which is the last) supplying the place of male,
The other of the female, in all metals.
Some do believe hermaphrodeity,
That both do act, and suffer. But, these two   165
Make the rest ductile, malleable, extensive.
And, even in gold, they are; for we do find
Seeds of them, by our fire, and gold in them:
And can produce the species of each metal
More perfect thence, than nature doth in earth.   170
Beside, who doth not see, in daily practice,
Art can beget bees, hornets, beetles, wasps,
Out of the carcasses, and dung of creatures;
Yea, scorpions, of an herb, being ritely placed:
And these are living creatures, far more perfect,   175
And excellent, than metals.

MAMMON   Well said, Father!

---

148   *propria materia* a specific substance
165   *do act, and suffer* are active and passive; this division of all things into active and
       passive, male and female, light and dark, accords with the ancient Chinese divisions of
       Yang and Yin
166   *extensive* able to be stretched out
169   *species* essence or form
172–3 *Art . . . creatures* this was widely believed
174   *ritely placed* Delrio has 'rite posita': 'placed in accordance with the rites'; an audience
       would only hear 'rightly'. The herb is basil
176   *metals* metall Q

Nay, if he take you in hand, sir, with an argument,
He'll bray you in a mortar.
SURLY　　　　　　　　Pray you, sir, stay.
Rather, than I'll be brayed, sir, I'll believe,
That alchemy is a pretty kind of game,　　　　　　　180
Somewhat like tricks o' the cards, to cheat a man,
With charming.
SUBTLE　　　　Sir?
SURLY　　　　　　　What else are all your terms,
Whereon no one o' your writers 'grees with other?
Of your elixir, your *lac virginis,*
Your stone, your med'cine, and your chrysosperm,　　185
Your sal, your sulphur, and your mercury,
Your oil of height, your tree of life, your blood,
Your marcasite, your tutty, your magnesia,
Your toad, your crow, your dragon, and your panther,
Your sun, your moon, your firmament, your adrop,　　190
Your lato, azoch, zernich, chibrit, heautarit,
And then, your red man, and your white woman,
With all your broths, your menstrues, and materials,
Of piss, and eggshells, women's terms, man's blood,
Hair o' the head, burnt clouts, chalk, merds, and clay,　195

178　*bray* pound
182–207　*What else . . . allegories* also from Delrio
185　*chrysosperm* seed of gold
187　*tree of life* Philosopher's Stone
　　blood redness
188　*marcasite* crystalised iron pirites
　　tutty impure zinc oxide (collected from chimneys)
189　*toad . . . crow . . . panther* all colours which appear at different stages of the work; the
　　dragon is mercury
190　*firmament* blue
　　adrop lead
191　*lato* latten; a compound similar to brass
　　azoch mercury (Arabic *az-zaug*)
　　zernich trisulphide of arsenic
　　chibrit sulphur
　　heautarit mercury
194　*eggshells* according to Aubrey, John Dee 'used to distill Egge-shells, and 'twas from hence
　　that Ben. Johnson had his hint of the *Alkimist*, whom he meant' *Brief Lives*, ed.
　　O. L. Dick, Harmondsworth, 1972, p. 249
　　women's terms menstrual blood
195　*clouts* rags
　　merds faeces

Powder of bones, scalings of iron, glass,
And worlds of other strange ingredients,
Would burst a man to name?

SUBTLE   And all these, named
Intending but one thing: which art our writers
Used to obscure their art.

MAMMON   Sir, so I told him,
Because the simple idiot should not learn it,   200
And make it vulgar.

SUBTLE   Was not all the knowledge
Of the Egyptians writ in mystic symbols?
Speak not the Scriptures, oft, in parables?
Are not the choicest fables of the poets,   205
That were the fountains, and first springs of wisdom,
Wrapped in perplexed allegories?

MAMMON   I urged that,
And cleared to him, that Sisyphus was damned
To roll the ceaseless stone, only, because
He would have made ours common.

DOL *is seen*

Who is this?   210

SUBTLE

God's precious – What do you mean? Go in, good lady,
Let me entreat you.   [*Exit* DOL]
Where's this varlet?

[*Enter* FACE]

FACE   Sir?
SUBTLE

You very knave! Do you use me, thus?
FACE   Wherein, sir?

201–7   *simple idiot . . . allegories* cf. Henry Reynolds on the rationale of hieroglyphs, 'that high
and Mysticall matters should by riddles and enigmaticall knotts be kept inuiolate from
the prophane Multitude', *Mythomystes in Critical Essays of the Seventeenth Century*, ed.
J. E. Spingarn, Oxford, 1957, vol. I, p. 156

208   *Sisyphus* condemned to an eternity of rolling a boulder up a hill in Hades; the boulder
always rolls back when the summit is reached

210   *common* this word punningly cues in Dol

SUBTLE
Go in, and see, you traitor. Go.   [*Exit* FACE]
MAMMON   Who is it, sir?
SUBTLE
Nothing, sir. Nothing.
MAMMON   What's the matter? Good, sir!   215
I have not seen you thus distempered. Who is 't?
SUBTLE
All arts have still had, sir, their adversaries,
But ours the most ignorant.

FACE *returns*

What now?
FACE
'Twas not my fault, sir, she would speak with you.
SUBTLE
Would she, sir? Follow me.   [*Exit* SUBTLE]
MAMMON   Stay, Lungs.
FACE   I dare not, sir   220
MAMMON
Stay man, what is she?
FACE   A lord's sister, sir.
MAMMON
How! Pray thee stay?
FACE   She's mad, sir, and sent hither—
(He'll be mad too.
MAMMON   I warrant thee.) Why sent hither?
FACE
Sir, to be cured.
SUBTLE [*within*] Why, rascal!
FACE   Lo you. Here, sir.   *He goes out*
MAMMON
'Fore God, a Bradamante, a brave piece.   225
SURLY
Heart, this is a bawdy-house! I'll be burnt else.

221–2 Q transposed in F
225 *Bradamante* a woman knight in Ariosto's *Orlando Furioso*

MAMMON

O, by this light, no. Do not wrong him. He's
Too scrupulous, that way. It is his vice.
No, he's a rare physician, do him right.
An excellent Paracelsian! And has done   230
Strange cures with mineral physic. He deals all
With spirits, he. He will not hear a word
Of Galen, or his tedious recipes.

[*Enter*] FACE *again*

How now, Lungs!
FACE   Softly, sir, speak softly. I meant
To ha' told your worship all. This must not hear.   235
MAMMON

No, he will not be gulled; let him alone.
FACE

You're very right, sir, she is a most rare scholar;
And is gone mad, with studying Broughton's works.
If you but name a word, touching the Hebrew,
She falls into her fit, and will discourse   240
So learnedly of genealogies,
As you would run mad, too, to hear her, sir.
MAMMON

How might one do t'have conference with her, Lungs?
FACE

O, divers have run mad upon the conference.
I do not know, sir: I am sent in haste,   245
To fetch a vial.
SURLY   Be not gulled, Sir Mammon.
MAMMON

Wherein? Pray ye, be patient.
SURLY   Yes, as you are.
And trust confederate knaves, and bawds, and whores.

---

230 *Paracelsian* a follower of Paracelsus (1493–1541) whose holistic medical theories involved
     the application of chemical principles. He was believed to have learned the secret of the
     Philosopher's Stone while in Constantinople
238 *Broughton* Hugh Broughton (1549–1612), a puritan and rabbinical scholar. His idiolect
     is referred to in *Volpone*: SIR POL. Is not his language rare? PER. But alchemy,/I never
     heard the like – or Broughton's books. (II.ii.118–20)
241 *genealogies* Broughton attempted to settle Old Testament chronology in *A Concent of
     Scripture*, 1590, from which Dol quotes in IV. v

MAMMON

    You are too foul, believe it. Come here, Ulen.

    One word.

FACE   I dare not, in good faith.

MAMMON   Stay, knave.   250

FACE

    He's extreme angry, that you saw her, sir.

MAMMON

    [*Gives money*] Drink that. What is she, when she's out of her fit?

FACE

    O, the most affablest creature, sir! So merry!

    So pleasant! She'll mount you up, like quicksilver,

    Over the helm; and circulate, like oil,   255

    A very vegetal: discourse of state,

    Of mathematics, bawdry, anything—

MAMMON

    Is she no way accessible? No means,

    No, trick, to give a man a taste of her – wit—

    Or so? Ulen!

FACE   I'll come to you again, sir,   [Exit FACE]   260

MAMMON

    Surly, I did not think, one o' your breeding

    Would traduce personages of worth.

SURLY   Sir Epicure,

    Your friend to use: yet, still, loth to be gulled.

    I do not like your philosophical bawds.

    Their stone is lechery enough, to pay for,   265

    Without this bait.

MAMMON   'Heart, you abuse yourself.

    I know the lady, and her friends, and means,

    The original of this disaster. Her brother

    Has told me all.

SURLY   And yet, you ne'er saw her

    Till now?

MAMMON   O, yes, but I forgot. I have (believe it)   270

249 *Ulen* Zephyrus Q
255 *helm* see II.i.98; the head of the penis is also implied
256 *vegetal* see I.i.39; here emphasis is on Dol's liveliness
259 *her-wit-/Or so* her-/Wit?or so Q
260 *Ulen* not in Q
268 *original* source

One of the treacherous'st memories, I do think,
Of all mankind.

SURLY   What call you her, brother?

MAMMON   My lord—
He wi' not have his name known, now I think on't.

SURLY

A very treacherous memory!

MAMMON   O' my faith—

SURLY

Tut, if you ha' it not about you, pass it,   275
Till we meet next.

MAMMON   Nay, by this hand, 'tis true.
He's one I honour, and my noble friend,
And I respect his house.

SURLY   Heart! Can it be,
That a grave sir, a rich, that has no need,
A wise sir, too, at other times, should thus   280
With his own oaths, and arguments, make hard means
To gull himself? And, this be your elixir,
Your *lapis mineralis*, and your lunary,
Give me your honest trick, yet, at primero,
Or gleek; and take your *lutum sapientis*,   285
Your *menstruum simplex*: I'll have gold, before you,
And, with less danger of the quicksilver;
Or the hot sulphur.

[*Enter* FACE]

FACE *to* SURLY   Here's one from Captain Face, sir,
Desires you meet him i' the Temple Church,

272 SURLY SVB. Q, F
275 *pass it* leave it
283 *lapis mineralis* mineral stone
     lunary the plant now known as honesty; in alchemy this would be associated with the
     moon's metal, silver
284 *primero* a card game; the best hand of four cards is the 'prime'
285 *gleek* a card game for three players
     lutum sapientis 'the philosopher's lute'– a quick-drying paste used to seal vessels quickly
286 *menstruum simplex* simple solvent
287–8 *less danger . . . sulphur* quicksilver was used in the treatment of venereal disease which Surly
     suggests Mammon is likely to contract in this place; sulphur is a remedy for skin infections
289 *Temple Church* the official church for law students and – like St. Paul's – a centre for
     gossip and meetings

Some half hour hence, and upon earnest business.   290
He whispers MAMMON

Sir, if you please to quit us, now; and come,
Again, within two hours: you shall have
My master busy examining o' the works;
And I will steal you in, unto the party,
That you may see her converse. [*To* SURLY] Sir, shall
 I say,   295
You'll meet the Captain's worship?
SURLY   Sir, I will.
(But, by attorney, and to a second purpose.
Now, I am sure, it is a bawdy house;
I'll swear it, were the Marshal here, to thank me:
The naming this Commander, doth confirm it.   300
Don Face! Why, he's the most authentic dealer
I' these commodities! The Superintendent
To all the quainter traffickers, in town.
He is their Visitor, and does appoint
Who lies with whom; and at what hour; what price;   305
Which gown; and in what smock; what fall; what tire.
Him will I prove, by a third person, to find
The subleties of this dark labyrinth:
Which if I do discover, dear Sir Mammon,
You'll give your poor friend leave, though no
 philosopher,   310
To laugh: for you that are, 'tis thought, shall weep.)
FACE
Sir. He does pray, you'll not forget.
SURLY   I will not, sir.
Sir Epicure, I shall leave you?
MAMMON   I follow you, straight.
[*Exit* SURLY]

FACE
But do so, good sir, to avoid suspicion.
This gent'man has a parlous head.

295 *converse* the word has a sexual sense
297 *by attorney* not in my own person
303 *quainter traffickers* prostitutes; 'quaint' used to mean cunt
306 *fall* falling band or veil
307 *prove* test (Lat. *probare*)

MAMMON   But wilt thou, Ulen.   315
Be constant to thy promise?
FACE   As my life, sir.
MAMMON
And wilt thou insinuate what I am? And praise me?
And say I am a noble fellow?
FACE   O, what else, sir?
And, that you'll make her royal, with the stone,
An Empress; and yourself King of Bantam.   320
MAMMON
Wilt thou do this?
FACE   Will I, sir?
MAMMON   Lungs, my Lungs!
I love thee.
FACE.   Send your stuff, sir, that my master
May busy himself, about projection.
MAMMON
Th'hast witched me, rogue: take, [*Gives money*] go.
FACE   Your jack, and all, sir.
MAMMON
Thou art a villain – I will send my jack;   325
And the weights too. Slave, I could bite thine ear.
Away, thou dost not care for me.
FACE   Not I, sir?
MAMMON
Come, I was born to make thee, my good weasel;
Set thee on a bench: and, ha' thee twirl a chain
With the best lord's vermin, of 'em all.
FACE   Away, sir.   330
MAMMON
A Count, nay, a Count Palatine—
FACE   Good sir, go.
MAMMON
—Shall not advance thee, better: no, nor faster.

                              [*Exit* MAMMON]

315 *parlous* difficult to deal with, risky, cunning
     Ulen not in Q
320 *Bantam* a city in north Java, once capital of a Mohammetan empire and
     legendary for its magnificence
324 *jack* a machine for turning a spit (driven by weights)
331 *Count Palatine* originally a count attached to an imperial palace with supreme judicial
     authority; later, a count permitted supreme jurisdiction of his province

Act II, Scene iv

[*Enter*] SUBTLE, DOL [*to* FACE]

SUBTLE
  Has he bit? Has he bit?
FACE   And swallowed too, my Subtle.
  I ha' given him line, and now he plays, i' faith.
SUBTLE
  And shall we twitch him?
FACE   Thorough both the gills.
  A wench is a rare bait, with which a man
  No sooner's taken, but he straight firks mad.   5
SUBTLE
  Dol, my Lord Whats'hum's sister, you must now
  Bear yourself statelich.
DOL   O, let me alone.
  I'll not forget my race, I warrant you.
  I'll keep my distance, laugh, and talk aloud;
  Have all the tricks of a proud scurvy lady,   10
  And be as rude's her woman.
FACE   Well said, Sanguine.
SUBTLE
  But will he send his andirons?
FACE   His jack too;
  And's iron shoeing-horn: I ha' spoke to him. Well,
  I must not lose my wary gamester, yonder.
SUBTLE
  O Monsieur Caution, that will not be gulled?   15
FACE
  Ay, if I can strike a fine hook into him, now,
  The Temple Church, there I have cast mine angle.
  Well, pray for me. I'll about it.

                              One knocks

2 *line . . . plays* the image is from angling
5 *firks mad* falls into transports of madness
7 *statelich* in a stately way (Dutch, or German); the Netherlands wars, in which Jonson
   served, brought many such words into England
11 *Sanguine* those in whom the sanguine (bloody) humour is predominant are optimistic,
   bold and amorous
17 *angle* fishing line

SUBTLE   What, more gudgeons!
   Dol, scout, scout; stay Face, you must go to the door:
   Pray God, it be my Anabaptist. Who is't, Dol?   20
DOL [*At window*]
   I know him not. He looks like a gold-end-man.
SUBTLE
   Gods so! 'Tis he, he said he would send. What call you him?
   The sanctified Elder, that should deal
   For Mammon's jack, and andirons! Let him in.
   Stay, help me off, first, with my gown. Away   25
   Madam, to your withdrawing chamber.   [*Exit* DOL]
                              Now,
   In a new tune, new gesture, but old language.
   This fellow is sent, from one negotiates with me
   About the stone, too; for the holy Brethren
   Of Amsterdam, the exiled Saints: that hope   30
   To raise their discipline, by it. I must use him
   In some strange fashion, now, to make him admire me.

Act II, Scene v

[*Enter*] ANANIAS [*to them*]

SUBTLE
   Where is my drudge?
FACE   Sir.
SUBTLE   Take away the recipient,
   And rectify your menstrue, from the phlegma.
   Then pour it, o' the Sol, in the cucurbite,
   And let 'em macerate, together.

---

  18 *gudgeons* small, freshwater fish, used as bait but themselves easily caught
  20 *Anabaptist* member of the non-conformist sect of Anabaptists who advocated adult
      baptism, community of goods and no authority other than the Scriptures. They
      originated on the Continent in the 1520s and began to arrive in England in the 1530s (in
      1535 a proclamation against their heresy was issued)
  21 *gold-end-man* a buyer and seller of old gold
29–30 *holy Brethren . . . Saints* the Anabaptists attempted to take control of several Dutch cities,
      including Amsterdam; they fled to England to escape the consequent persecutions

   2 *phlegma* watery distillate
   4 *macerate* soften by soaking

FACE   Yes, sir.
  And save the ground?
SUBTLE   No. *Terra damnata*   5
  Must not have entrance, in the work. Who are you?
ANANIAS
  A faithful Brother, if it please you.
SUBTLE   What's that?
  A Lullianist? A Ripley? *Filius artis*?
  Can you sublime, and dulcify? Calcine?
  Know you the *sapor pontic*? *Sapor styptic*?   10
  Or, what is homogene, or heterogene?
ANANIAS
  I understand no heathen language, truly.
SUBTLE
  Heathen, you Knipper-Doling? Is *Ars sacra*,
  Or *chrysopoeia*, or *spagyrica*,
  Or the pamphysic, or panarchic knowledge,   15
  A heathen language?
ANANIAS   Heathen Greek, I take it.
SUBTLE
  How? Heathen Greek?
ANANIAS   All's heathen, but the Hebrew.

5 *the ground* the sediment which remains after distillation
   Terra damnata damned earth
8 *Lullianist* follower of Raymond Lull (1235–1315), Spanish missionary, deviser of mnemonic
   schemes and (reputedly) alchemist; many alchemical works are attributed to him
   Ripley follower of George Ripley (d. *c.* 1490), author of *The Compound of Alchemy* (in
   T.C.B.); he did much to popularise in England works attributed to Lull
   Filius artis a 'son of the art' (Lat.); Subtle pretends to misunderstand Ananias' description
   of himself as 'A faithful Brother'
9 *dulcify* sweeten by dissolving the salt from a substance
10 *sapor pontic . . . Sapor styptic* nine 'sapors' (tastes) were distinguished by alchemists; five
   are created by heat and four (including pontic and stiptic) by cold
   styptick stipstick Q, F
13 *Knipper-Doling* Bernard Knipperdollinck was a leading Anabaptist and instrumental in
   the occupation of Münster in 1534 where the Anabaptists established a 'Kingdom of God'
   under the rule of John of Leyden
   Ars sacra the sacred art
14 *chrysopoeia* gold-making (Greek)
   spagyrica a word supposedly coined by Paracelsus from the Greek σπαω (to stretch and
   rend) and αγειρω (to collect together); it signifies the Paracelsian method of alchemy
   by separation and combination
15 *pamphysic, or panarchic knowledge* knowledge of all nature or all power
17 *All's heathen, but the Hebrew* Hebrew was believed by some to be the unfallen language
   that Adam first used

SUBTLE

    Sirrah, my varlet, stand you forth, and speak to him
    Like a philosopher: answer, i' the language.
    Name the vexations, and the martyrizations   20
    Of metals, in the work.

FACE   Sir, Putrefaction,

    Solution, Ablution, Sublimation,
    Cohobation, Calcination, Ceration, and
    Fixation.

SUBTLE   This is heathen Greek, to you, now?

    And when comes Vivification?

FACE   After Mortification.   25

SUBTLE

    What's Cohobation?

FACE   'Tis the pouring on

    Your *Aqua Regis,* and then drawing him off,
    To the trine circle of the seven spheres.

SUBTLE

    What's the proper passion of metals?

FACE   Malleation.

SUBTLE

    What's your *ultimum supplicium auri?*

FACE   *Antimonium.*   30

SUBTLE

    This 's heathen Greek, to you? And, what's your
       mercury?

19 *i' the language* in the language of alchemy
20 *vexations* contortions
    martyrizations various processes of reduction to which the metals are subjected; the metaphor suits the hearer
21 *Putrefaction* breaking down
    Ablution washing
23 *Cohobation* repeated distillation
    Ceration see II.iii.84
25 *Vivification* the process of extracting a pure substance from a compound
    Mortification breaking down of substance
27 *Aqua Regis* 'King's Water'; a mixture of vitriol and hydrochloric acid; it is so named because it is able to dissolve the 'noble' metals
28 *the trine circle of the seven spheres:* 'Know, too, that no solution will take place in your electrum unless it thrice runs perfectly through the sphere of seven planets'. *The Hermetic and Alchemical Writings of Paracelsus*, ed. A. E. Waite, 2 vols, London 1894, vol. ii, p. 105
29 *passion* again, the religious dimension of this word fits it to the hearer
30 *ultimum supplicium auri* extreme punishment for gold
    Antimonium antimony – a slight alloy which destroys the malleability of gold

FACE
  A very fugitive, he will be gone, sir.
SUBTLE
  How know you him?
FACE   By his viscosity,
  His oleosity, and his suscitability.
SUBTLE
  How do you sublime him?
FACE   With the calce of eggshells,   35
  White marble, talc.
SUBTLE   Your *magisterium*, now?
  What's that?
FACE   Shifting, sir, your elements,
  Dry into cold, cold into moist, moist in –
  To hot, hot into dry.
SUBTLE   This 's heathen Greek to you, still?
  Your *lapis philosophicus?*
FACE   'Tis a stone, and not   40
  A stone; a spirit, a soul, and a body:
  Which, if you do dissolve, it is dissolved,
  If you coagulate, it is coagulated,
  If you make it to fly, it flieth.
SUBTLE   Enough   [*Exit* FACE]
  This 's heathen Greek, to you? What are you, sir?   45
ANANIAS
  Please you, a servant of the exiled Brethren,
  That deal with widows' and with orphans' goods;
  And make a just account, unto the Saints:
  A Deacon.
SUBTLE   O, you are sent from master Wholesome,
  Your teacher?
ANANIAS   From Tribulation Wholesome,   50
  Our very zealous Pastor.

---

  34   *oleosity* oiliness
       suscitability excitability
  35   *calce* calx (i.e. powder)
  37–9 *Shifting . . . dry* F. H. Mares (in the Revels edition of the play) suggests that this may be
       the 'philosopher's wheel' of II.iii.44. The process involves placing substances into their
       opposing elements in order to reduce them to their essences
  48   *Saints* Ananias is anticipating the mass canonization of the brethren

SUBTLE   Good. I have
  Some orphans' goods to come here.
ANANIAS   Of what kind, sir?
SUBTLE
  Pewter, and brass, andirons, and kitchen ware,
  Metals, that we must use our med'cine on:
  Wherein the Brethren may have a penn'orth,   55
  For ready money.
ANANIAS   Were the orphans' parents
  Sincere professors?
SUBTLE   Why do you ask?
ANANIAS   Because
  We then are to deal justly, and give (in truth)
  Their utmost value.
SUBTLE   'Slid, you'd cozen, else,
  And, if their parents were not of the faithful?   60
  I will not trust you, now I think on 't,
  Till I ha' talked with your Pastor. Ha you brought
      money
  To buy more coals?
ANANIAS   No, surely.
SUBTLE   No? How so?
ANANIAS
  The Brethren bid me say unto you, sir.
  Surely, they will not venture any more   65
  Till they may see projection.
SUBTLE   How!
ANANIAS   You've had,
  For the instruments, as bricks, and loam, and glasses,
  Already thirty pound; and, for materials,
  They say, some ninety more: and, they have heard, since,
  That one, at Heidelberg, made it, of an egg,   70
  And a small paper of pin-dust.
SUBTLE   What's your name?

---

57 *professors* of the Anabaptist faith
70 *Heidelberg* believed to be the centre of alchemy
71 *pin-dust* metallic dust produced in the manufacture of pins (Germany was ahead of
    England in this; pins were not produced in England until 1626)

ANANIAS
　My name is Ananias.
SUBTLE　　　　　　　Out, the varlet
　That cozened the Apostles! Hence, away,
　Flee Mischief; had your holy Consistory
　No name to send me, of another sound;　　　　　　　　75
　Than wicked Ananias? Send your Elders,
　Hither, to make atonement for you, quickly.
　And gi' me satisfaction; or out goes
　The fire: and down th' alembics, and the furnace,
　Piger Henricus, or what not. Thou wretch,　　　　　80
　Both Sericon, and Bufo, shall be lost,
　Tell 'em. All hope of rooting out the Bishops,
　Or th' Antichristian Hierarchy shall perish,
　If they stay threescore minutes. The Aqueity,
　Terreity, and Sulphureity　　　　　　　　　　　85
　Shall run together again, and all be annulled,
　Thou wicked Ananias.　　　　　[*Exit* ANANIAS]
　　　　　　　　This will fetch 'em,
　And make 'em haste towards their gulling more.
　A man must deal like a rough nurse, and fright
　Those, that are froward, to an appetite.　　　　　90

Act II, Scene vi

[*Enter*] DRUGGER, FACE [*dressed as Captain to* SUBTLE]

FACE
　He's busy with his spirits, but we'll upon him.
SUBTLE
　How now! What mates? What Bayards ha' we here?

72–3　*Ananias . . . Apostles* see *Acts* v 1–11
　74　*Consistory* assembly
　76　*Elders* high-ranking church officers
　80　*Piger Henricus* a 'lazy Henry': a multiple furnace fired by a single, central fire
　81　*Sericon, and Bufo* red and black tincture ('Bufo' is 'the toad')
72–3　*All hope . . . Hierarchy* many saw the retention of bishops in the Church of England as a
　　　residue of popery
84–6　*The Aqueity . . . annulled* all the work of separation and purification will be undone
　90　*froward* hard to please

　2　*Bayards* Bayard was a common name for a horse (see Chaucer, *Troilus and Criseyde* I, 218

FACE

    I told you, he would be furious. Sir, here's Nab,

    Has brought you another piece of gold, to look on:

    [*To* DRUGGER] (We must appease him. Give it me) and prays you,   5

    You would devise (what is it Nab?)

DRUGGER   A sign, sir.

FACE

    Ay, a good lucky one, a thriving sign, Doctor.

SUBTLE

    I was devising now.

FACE [*To* SUBTLE]   ('Slight, do not say so,

    He will repent he ga' you any more.)

    What say you to his constellation, Doctor?   10

    The Balance?

SUBTLE   No, that way is stale, and common.

    A townsman, born in Taurus, gives the bull;

    Or the bull's head: in Aries, the ram.

    A poor device. No, I will have his name

    Formed in some mystic character; whose radii,   15

    Striking the senses of the passers-by,

    Shall, by a virtual influence, breed affections,

    That may result upon the party owns it:

    As thus—

FACE   Nab!

SUBTLE   He first shall have a bell, that's Abel;

    And, by it, standing one, whose name is Dee,   20

    In a rug gown; there's D and Rug, that's Drug:

    And, right anenst him, a dog snarling *Er*;

    There's Drugger, Abel Drugger. That's his sign.

    And here's now mystery, and hieroglyphic.

---

  11 *Balance* Libra

  12 *gives* uses as his sign

  15 *radii* emanations

  17 *virtual influence* influence of its power

        affections inclinations

19–24 Subtle is constructing a rebus of Drugger's name. Rebuses (which originated in France)
      were popular at the time. Camden mentions a man who expressed 'Rose Hill I
      love well' by painting the border of his gown with a rose, a hill, a loaf and a
      well (*Remains*, 1623, p. 145)

  20 *Dee* John Dee (1527–1608); an eminent occultist patronised by Queen Elizabeth

FACE
    Abel, thou art made.
DRUGGER   Sir, I do thank his worship   [*Bows*]   25
FACE
    Six o' thy legs more, will not do it, Nab.
    He has brought you a pipe of tobacco, Doctor.
DRUGGER   Yes, sir:
    I have another thing, I would impart—
FACE
    Out with it, Nab.
DRUGGER   Sir, there is lodged, hard by me,
    A rich young widow—
FACE   Good! A *bona roba*?   30
DRUGGER
    But nineteen, at the most.
FACE   Very good, Abel.
DRUGGER
    Marry, she's not in fashion, yet; she wears
    A hood: but 't stands a cop.
FACE   No matter, Abel.
DRUGGER
    And, I do, now and then give her a fucus—
FACE
    What! Dost thou deal, Nab?
SUBTLE   I did tell you, Captain.   35
DRUGGER
    And physic too sometime, sir: for which she trusts me
    With all her mind. She's come up here, of purpose
    To learn the fashion.
FACE   Good (his match too!) on, Nab.
DRUGGER
    And she does strangely long to know her fortune.
FACE
    God's lid, Nab, send her to the Doctor, hither.   40

---

    25 FACE not in Q
    26 *legs* bows
    30 *bona roba* fine woman; prostitute
    33 *a cop* on the head (a hat would have been more fashionable than a hood, but at least she wears her hood *like* a hat)
    34 *fucus* a cosmetic; Face pretends to understand 'fuck'
    35 *deal* do business (with sexual sense of 'get down to it')

DRUGGER
    Yes, I have spoke to her of his worship, already:
    But she's afraid, it will be blown abroad
    And hurt her marriage.
FACE   Hurt it? 'Tis the way
    To heal it, if 'twere hurt; to make it more
    Followed, and sought: Nab, thou shalt tell her this.   45
    She'll be more known, more talked of, and your widows
    Are ne'er of any price till they be famous;
    Their honour is their multitude of suitors:
    Send her, it may be thy good fortune. What?
    Thou dost not know.
DRUGGER   No, sir, she'll never marry   50
    Under a knight. Her brother has made a vow.
FACE
    What, and dost thou despair, my little Nab,
    Knowing, what the Doctor has set down for thee,
    And, seeing so many, o' the city, dubbed?
    One glass o' thy water, with a Madam, I know,   55
    Will have it done, Nab. What's her brother? A knight?
DRUGGER
    No, sir, a gentleman, newly warm in his land, sir,
    Scarce cold in his one and twenty; that does govern
    His sister, here: and is a man himself
    Of some three thousand a year, and is come up   60
    To learn to quarrel, and to live by his wits,
    And will go down again, and die i' the country.
FACE
    How! To quarrel?
DRUGGER   Yes, sir, to carry quarrels,
    As gallants do, and manage 'em, by line.
FACE
    'Slid, Nab! The Doctor is the only man   65
    In Christendom for him. He has made a table,
    With mathematical demonstrations,
    Touching the art of quarrels. He will give him
    An instrument to quarrel by. Go, bring 'em, both:

54   *dubbed* knighted; James I notoriously raised money by selling knighthoods to the new rich
57   *newly warm in* who has just gained
64   *by line* by rules
66   *table* diagram, visual scheme

Him, and his sister. And, for thee, with her   70
The Doctor haply may persuade. Go to.
Shalt give his worship, a new damask suit
Upon the premises.
SUBTLE   O, good Captain.
FACE   He shall,
He is the honestest fellow, Doctor, Stay not,
No offers, bring the damask, and the parties.   75
DRUGGER
I'll try my power, sir.
FACE   And thy will too, Nab.
SUBTLE
'Tis good tobacco this! What is't an ounce?
FACE
He'll send you a pound, Doctor.
SUBTLE   O, no.
FACE   He will do't.
It is the goodest soul. Abel, about it.
(Thou shalt know more anon. Away, be gone.)   80

                                        [*Exit* DRUGGER]

A miserable rogue, and lives with cheese,
And has the worms. That was the cause indeed
Why he came now. He dealt with me, in private,
To get a med'cine for 'em.
SUBTLE   And shall, sir. This works.
FACE
A wife, a wife, for one on's, my dear Subtle: 85
We'll e'en draw lots, and he, that fails, shall have
The more in goods, the other has in tail.
SUBTLE
Rather the less. For she may be so light
She may want grains.
FACE   Ay, or be such a burden,
A man would scarce endure her, for the whole.   90

74 *Stay not* Say not Q
85 *on's* of us
87 *in tail* puns on 1) genital satisfaction ('tail' is still used in this sense) and 2)entail – a
    settlement of succession to an estate
89 *grains* a grain is the smallest unit of weight, based upon a grain of corn or wheat

SUBTLE

Faith, best let's see her first, and then determine.

FACE

Content. But Dol must ha' no breath on't.

SUBTLE   Mum.

Away, you to your Surly yonder, catch him.

FACE

Pray God, I ha' not stayed too long.

SUBTLE   I fear it.   [*Exeunt*]

Act III, Scene i

[*In the street outside Lovewit's house*]

[*Enter*] TRIBULATION, ANANIAS

TRIBULATION

These chastisements are common to the Saints,
And such rebukes we of the Separation
Must bear, with willing shoulders, as the trials
Sent forth, to tempt our frailties.

ANANIAS   In pure zeal,

I do not like the man: he is a heathen.   5
And speaks the language of Canaan, truly.

TRIBULATION

I think him a profane person, indeed.

ANANIAS   He bears

The visible mark of the Beast, in his forehead.
And for his stone, it is a work of darkness,
And, with philosophy, blinds the eyes of man.   10

TRIBULATION

Good Brother, we must bend unto all means,
That may give furtherance, to the holy cause.

2–4 *we of the . . . Sent forth* th'Elect must beare, with patience;/They are the exercises of the Spirit,/And sent Q

2 *Separation* the Anabaptists believed themselves to be the elect, separate from all others

6 *the language of Canaan* as opposed to Hebrew or their Puritan idiolect; 'In that day shall five cities in the land of Egypt speak the language of Canaan', *Isaiah* xix.18

8 *mark of the Beast Revelation* xvi.2, xix.20 .

ANANIAS
    Which his cannot: the sanctified cause
    Should have a sanctified course.

TRIBULATION   Not always necessary.
    The children of perdition are, oft-times,   15
    Made instruments even of the greatest works.
    Beside, we should give somewhat to man's nature,
    The place he lives in, still about the fire,
    And fume of metals, that intoxicate
    The brain of man, and make him prone to passion.   20
    Where have you greater atheists, than your cooks?
    Or more profane, or choleric than your glassmen?
    More antichristian, than your bell-founders?
    What makes the Devil so devilish, I would ask you,
    Satan, our common enemy, but his being   25
    Perpetually about the fire, and boiling
    Brimstone, and arsenic? We must give, I say,
    Unto the motives, and the stirrers up
    Of humours in the blood. It may be so.
    When as the work is done, the stone is made,   30
    This heat of his may turn into a zeal,
    And stand up for the beauteous discipline,
    Against the menstruous cloth, and rag of Rome.
    We must await his calling, and the coming
    Of the good spirit. You did fault, t' upbraid him   35
    With the Brethren's blessing of Heidelberg, weighing
    What need we have, to hasten on the work,
    For the restoring of the silenced Saints,
    Which ne'er will be, but by the philosopher's stone.
    And, so a learned Elder, one of Scotland,   40

15–16 *The children . . . works* this concept of evil being, in spite of itself, an agent for good was a familiar one. Shakespeare's Richard III is an example

17 *give* concede

18 *still* always

33 *rag of Rome* the Puritans identified the Church of Rome with the scarlet clad woman of *Revelation* xvii. Here the red surplice worn by Roman bishops is identified with rags stained with menstrual blood. The alchemists also used a *menstruum*; the words could be taken in three different ways (alchemical, theological, gynaecological) according to the situation of the hearer

38 *the silenced Saints* puritan clergy excommunicated for non-conformity after the Hampton Court conference of 1604; they were known as the 'silenced ministers'

Assured me; *aurum potabile* being
The only med'cine, for the civil magistrate,
T' incline him to a feeling of the cause:
And must be daily used, in the disease.

ANANIAS

I have not edified more, truly, by man;   45
Not since the beautiful light, first, shone on me:
And I am sad, my zeal hath so offended.

TRIBULATION

Let us call on him, then.

ANANIAS   The motion's good,
And of the spirit; I will knock first: [*Knocks*]
                              Peace be within.

Act III, Scene ii

[*Inside Lovewit's house*]

[*Enter*] SUBTLE

SUBTLE

O, are you come? 'Twas time. Your threescore minutes
Were at the last thread, you see; and down had gone
Furnus acediae, turris circulatorius:
Lembic, bolt's head, retort, and pelican
Had all been cinders. Wicked Ananias!   5
Art thou returned? Nay then, it goes down, yet.

TRIBULATION

Sir, be appeased, he is come to humble
Himself in spirit, and to ask your patience,
If too much zeal hath carried him, aside,
From the due path.

SUBTLE   Why, this doth qualify!   10

---

41 *aurum potabile* drinkable gold; bribery is intended here
48 *motion* intention

3   *Furnus acediae* 'the furnace of sloth'; the same as the 'lazy Henry' of II.v.80
    turris circulatorius circulating tower; an apparatus for continuous circulation and
    refinement
4   *Lembic* alembic
10 *qualify* mitigate

TRIBULATION
    The Brethren had no purpose, verily,
    To give you the least grievance: but are ready
    To lend their willing hands, to any project
    The spirit, and you direct.
SUBTLE   This qualifies more!
TRIBULATION
    And, for the orphans' goods, let them be valued,   15
    Or what is needful, else, to the holy work,
    It shall be numbered: here, by me, the Saints
    Throw down their purse before you.
SUBTLE   This qualifies, most!
    Why, thus it should be, now you understand.
    Have I discoursed so unto you, of our stone?   20
    And, of the good that it shall bring your cause?
    Showed you, (beside the main of hiring forces
    Abroad, drawing the Hollanders, your friends,
    From th' Indies, to serve you, with all their fleet)
    That even the mèd'cinal use shall make you a faction,   25
    And party in the realm? As, put the case,
    That some great man in state, he have the gout,
    Why, you but send three drops of your elixir,
    You help him straight: there you have made a friend.
    Another has the palsy, or the dropsy,   30
    He takes of your incombustible stuff,
    He's young again: there you have made a friend.
    A lady, that is past the feat of body,
    Though not of mind, and hath her face decayed
    Beyond all cure of paintings, you restore   35
    With the oil of talc; there you have made a friend:
    And all her friends. A lord, that is a leper,
    A knight, that has the bone-ache, or a squire
    That hath both these, you make 'em smooth, and sound,

---

17 *by me* in my person;
25–6 *That even . . . realm* you'll become a force to be reckoned with in the country merely
       through the influence you'll gain from its medical effects
33 *feat of body* copulation
35 *paintings* cosmetics; painting Q
36 *oil of talc* white elixir used by alchemists; this contrasts with the cosmetic used to whiten
       the skin

With a bare fricace of your medicine: still,   40
You increase your friends.

TRIBULATION   Ay, 'tis very pregnant.

SUBTLE
And, then, the turning of this lawyer's pewter
To plate, at Christmas—

ANANIAS   Christ-tide, I pray you.

SUBTLE
Yet, Ananias?

ANANIAS   I have done.

SUBTLE   Or changing
His parcel gilt, to massy gold. You cannot   45
But raise your friends. Withal, to be of power
To pay an army, in the field, to buy
The king of France, out of his realms; or Spain,
Out of his Indies: what can you not do,
Against lords spiritual, or temporal,   50
That shall oppone you?

TRIBULATION   Verily, 'tis true.
We may be temporal lords, ourselves, I take it.

SUBTLE
You may be anything, and leave off to make
Long-winded exercises: or suck up,
Your ha, and hum, in a tune. I not deny,   55
But such as are not graced, in a state,
May, for their ends, be adverse in religion,
And get a tune, to call the flock together:
For (to say sooth) a tune does much, with women,
And other phlegmatic people, it is your bell.   60

ANANIAS
Bells are profane: a tune may be religious.

SUBTLE
No warning with you? Then, farewell my patience.
'Slight, it shall down: I will not be thus tortured.

---

40 *fricace* rubbing
41 *pregnant* persuasive; full of sense
45 *parcel gilt* partly gilded stuff
51 *oppone* oppose
55 *I not* I do not
61 *Bells are profane* bells had popish associations
63 *it shall down* i.e. the alchemical apparatus

TRIBULATION
I pray you, sir.
SUBTLE   All shall perish. I have spoke it.
TRIBULATION
Let me find grace, sir, in your eyes; the man   65
He stands corrected: neither did his zeal
(But as yourself) allow a tune, somewhere.
Which, now, being toward the stone, we shall not need.
SUBTLE
No, nor your holy vizard, to win widows
To give you legacies; or make zealous wives   70
To rob their husbands, for the common cause:
Nor take the start of bonds, broke but one day,
And say, they were forfeited, by providence.
Nor shall you need, o'er-night, to eat huge meals,
To celebrate your next day's fast the better: 75
The whilst the Brethren, and the Sisters, humbled,
Abate the stiffness of the flesh. Nor cast
Before your hungry hearers, scrupulous bones,
As whether a Christian may hawk, or hunt;
Or whether, matrons, of the holy assembly,   80
May lay their hair out, or wear doublets:
Or have that idol Starch, about their linen.
ANANIAS
It is, indeed, an idol.

69–97 *No, nor . . . the Disciple* Subtle continues to expose the Anabaptists' craft and hypocrisy
to the audience while Ananias and Tribulation remain oblivious

69 *holy vizard* pious appearance

72 *take the start* take advantage of

77 *Abate the stiffness of the flesh* we (but not Ananias and Tribulation) should hear the sexual
innuendo here

78 *scrupulous bones* trivial bones of contention

79 *hawk . . . hunt* 'I neuer read of any, in *the* volume of *the* sacred scripture, that was a good
man and a Hunter'; Stubbes, *The Anatomie of the Abuses in England in Shakespeare's
Youth,* ed. Furnivall, 1877–9, part i, p. 181

81 *lay their hair out, or wear doublets* 'Then followeth the trimming and tricking of their
heds in laying out their hair to the shewe, which of force must be curled, frisled and
crisped, laid out (a World to see!) on wreathes & borders from one eare to an other' (ibid.
p. 67) and (re. *Deuteronomy* xxii 5) 'The Women also there haue dublets & Ierkins, as
men haue heer . . . & though this be a kinde of attire appropriate onely to man, yet they
blush not to wear it' (ibid. p. 73)

82 *that idol Starch* 'The deuils liquore, I mean *Starch*' (ibid. p. 70)

TRIBULATION   Mind him not, sir.
I do command thee, spirit (of zeal, but trouble)
To peace within him. Pray you, sir, go on.   85
SUBTLE
Nor shall you need to libel 'gainst the prelates,
And shorten so your ears, against the hearing
Of the next wire-drawn grace. Nor, of necessity,
Rail against plays, to please the alderman,
Whose daily custard you devour. Nor lie   90
With zealous rage, till you are hoarse. Not one
Of these so singular arts. Nor call yourselves,
By names of Tribulation, Persecution,
Restraint, Long-Patience, and such like, affected
By the whole family, or wood of you,   95
Only for glory, and to catch the ear
Of the disciple.
TRIBULATION   Truly, sir, they are
Ways, that the godly Brethren have invented,
For propagation of the glorious cause,
As very notable means, and whereby, also,   100
Themselves grow soon, and profitably famous.
SUBTLE
O, but the stone, all's idle to it! Nothing!
The art of angels, nature's miracle,
The divine secret, that doth fly in clouds,
From east to west: and whose tradition   105
Is not from men, but spirits.
ANANIAS   I hate traditions:
I do not trust 'em—
TRIBULATION   Peace.
ANANIAS   They are Popish, all.
I will not peace. I will not—
TRIBULATION   Ananias.

84–5 *I do . . . him* Tribulation is attempting to placate the troubled spirit that possesses Ananias
  87 *shorten so your ears* have your ears cut off or clipped as a punishment
  88 *wire-drawn grace* extended prayer (grace) before eating
  90 *custard* a kind of open pie; a bit like *quiche*
  95 *wood* a gathering of family trees; 'wood' also meant 'mad'– a good collective noun for extremists
  99 *glorious* holy Q
 106 *I hate traditions* some Puritans recognised only the authority of the Bible and direct revelation. Traditions were associated with the Church of Rome and Judaism

ANANIAS

    Please the profane, to grieve the godly: I may not.

SUBTLE

    Well, Ananias, thou shalt overcome.   110

TRIBULATION

    It is an ignorant zeal, that haunts him, sir.

    But truly, else, a very faithful Brother,

    A botcher: and a man, by revelation,

    That hath a competent knowledge of the truth.

SUBTLE

    Has he a competent sum, there, i' the bag,   115

    To buy the goods, within? I am made guardian,

    And must, for charity, and conscience' sake,

    Now, see the most be made, for my poor orphan:

    Though I desire the Brethren, too, good gainers.

    There, they are, within. When you have viewed, and bought 'em,   120

    And ta'en the inventory of what they are,

    They are ready for projection; there's no more

    To do: cast on the med'cine, so much silver

    As there is tin there, so much gold as brass,

    I'll gi' it you in, by weight.

TRIBULATION   But how long time,   125

    Sir, must the Saints expect, yet?

SUBTLE   Let me see,

    How's the moon, now? Eight, nine, ten days hence

    He will be silver potate; then, three days,

    Before he citronize: some fifteen days,

    The *magisterium* will be perfected.   130

ANANIAS

    About the second day, of the third week,

    In the ninth month?

SUBTLE   Yes, my good Ananias.

TRIBULATION

    What will the orphans' goods arise to, think you?

---

113 *botcher* probably used in the specialised sense of 'tailor'; John of Leyden, the
     Anabaptist 'King', had been a tailor and is called 'the botcher' by Thomas Nashe in his
     description of the occupation of Münster in *The Unfortunate Traveller*, ed. J. B. Steane,
     Harmondsworth, 1972, p. 277

128 *silver potate* liquid silver

129 *citronize* turn yellow – a sign that the work is near completion

SUBTLE

    Some hundred marks; as much as filled three cars,

    Unladed now: you'll make six millions of 'em   135

    But I must ha' more coals laid in.

TRIBULATION   How!

SUBTLE   Another load,

    And then we ha' finished. We must now increase

    Our fire to *ignis ardens*, we are past

    Fimus equinus, balnei, cineris,

    And all those lenter heats. If the holy purse   140

    Should, with this draught, fall low, and that the Saints

    Do need a present sum, I have a trick

    To melt the pewter, you shall buy now, instantly,

    And, with a tincture, make you as good Dutch dollars,

    As any are in Holland.

TRIBULATION   Can you so?   145

SUBTLE

    Ay, and shall bide the third examination.

ANANIAS

    It will be joyful tidings to the Brethren.

SUBTLE

    But you must carry it, secret.

TRIBULATION   Ay, but stay,

    This act of coining, is it lawful?

ANANIAS   Lawful?

    We know no magistrate. Or, if we did,   150

    This 's foreign coin.

SUBTLE   It is no coining, sir.

    It is but casting.

TRIBULATION   Ha? You distinguish well.

    Casting of money may be lawful.

---

134 *cars* carts

135 *you'll* you shall Q

138 *ignis ardens* the hottest fire

139 *Fimus equinus* the lowest form of heat, produced by horse dung

      balnei see II.iii.41

      cineris the heat of ashes

140 *lenter* slower

142 *have a trick* F2 have trick Q, F

150 *We know no magistrate* some Puritans would only accept Scriptural authority in civil matters

151–2 *It is . . . casting* the casting of foreign coin *was* as much an offence as coming English counterfeits (1 & 2 Philip and Mary, cxi)

ANANIAS   'Tis, sir.

TRIBULATION

Truly, I take it so.

SUBTLE   There is no scruple,

Sir, to be made of it; believe Ananias: 155

This case of conscience he is studied in.

TRIBULATION

I'll make a question of it, to the Brethren.

ANANIAS

The Brethren shall approve it lawful, doubt not.

Where shall't be done.

                              Knock without

SUBTLE   For that we'll talk, anon.

There's some to speak with me. Go in, I pray you,   160

And view the parcels. That's the inventory.

I'll come to you straight.

                    [*Exeunt* ANANIAS, TRIBULATION]

                    Who is it? Face! Appear.

Act III, Scene iii

[*Enter*] FACE [*dressed as Captain, to* SUBTLE]

SUBTLE

How now? Good prize?

FACE   Good pox! Yond' costive cheater

Never came on.

SUBTLE   How then?

FACE   I ha' walked the round,

Till now, and no such thing.

SUBTLE   And ha' you quit him?

FACE

Quit him? And hell would quit him too, he were happy.

'Slight, would you have me stalk like a mill-jade,   5

All day, for one, that will not yield us grains?

I know him of old

SUBTLE   O, but to ha' gulled him,

---

2 *walked the round* gone round the nave (of the Temple Church – also known as 'the round')

5 *mill-jade* a horse that works a mill by moving in circles

[103]

Had been a mastery.

FACE   Let him go, black boy,
And turn thee, that some fresh news may possess thee.
A noble Count, a Don of Spain (my dear   10
Delicious compeer, and my party-bawd)
Who is come hither, private, for his conscience,
And brought munition with him, six great slops,
Bigger than three Dutch hoys, beside round trunks
Furnished with pistolets, and pieces of eight,   15
Will straight be here, my rogue, to have thy bath
(That is the colour,) and to make his battery
Upon our Dol, our castle, our Cinque-Port,
Our Dover pier, our what thou wilt. Where is she?
She must prepare perfumes, delicate linen,   20
The bath in chief, a banquet, and her wit,
For she must milk his epididimis.
Where is the doxy?

SUBTLE   I'll send her to thee:
And but dispatch my brace of little John Leydens,
And come again myself.

FACE   Are they within then?   25

SUBTLE
Numbering the sum.

FACE   How much?

SUBTLE   A hundred marks, boy.

                                        [*Exit* SUBTLE]

8   *black boy* Subtle's face is darkened by the smoke of his business
9   *turn thee* shift your attention
11   *compeer* companion; mate
     party-bawd part bawd, or 'bawd of my party'
13   *slops* wide breeches
14   *hoys* small sea vessels carrying passengers and goods around coastal waters
     trunks trunk hose; knee breeches
15   *pistolets* Spanish gold coins
     pieces of eight Spanish dollars
18–19 *Cinque-Port . . . Dover pier* one of the five ports on the South-East coast of England
     occupying vital defence positions. Dover is the chief. Dol is a Cinque-Port because she
     is constantly invaded. The portals of her body and five senses may also be implied.
     'Cinque' would have been pronounced 'sink'
22   *milk* feele Q
     epididimis 'A long narrow structure attached to the posterior border of the adjoining
     outer surface of the testicle' (*OED*); so 'milk his epididimis' = 'drain his balls'
24   *John Leydens* John Leyden led the Anabaptist occupation of Münster in 1532–6

FACE

 Why, this 's a lucky day! Ten pounds of Mammon!
 Three o' my clerk! A portague o' my grocer!
 This o' the Brethren! Beside reversions,
 And states, to come i' the widow, and my Count!   30

      [*Enter* DOL]

 My share, today, will not be bought for forty—
DOL   What?
FACE

 Pounds, dainty Dorothy, art thou so near?
DOL

 Yes, say lord General, how fares our camp?
FACE

 As, with the few, that had entrenched themselves
 Safe, by their discipline, against a world, Dol: 35
 And laughed, within those trenches, and grew fat
 With thinking on the booties, Dol, brought in
 Daily, by their small parties. This dear hour,
 A doughty Don is taken, with my Dol;
 And thou may'st make his ransom, what thou wilt,   40
 My Dousabell: he shall be brought here, fettered
 With thy fair looks, before he sees thee; and thrown
 In a down-bed, as dark as any dungeon;
 Where thou shalt keep him waking, with thy drum;
 Thy drum, my Dol; thy drum; till he be tame   45
 As the poor blackbirds were i' the great frost,
 Or bees are with a basin: and so hive him
 I' the swanskin coverlid, and cambric sheets,
 Till he work honey, and wax, my little God's-gift.

---

29 *reversions* goods due in the future
33 *say . . . camp* the first line of Kyd's *The Spanish Tragedy* – a hugely popular play to which
  Jonson had written additions
41 *Dousabell* (French) 'douce et belle': sweet and lovely
44 *drum* belly; perhaps also suggesting the beat of sexual intercourse
46 *the great frost* of 1607–8 when the Thames froze over; the blackbirds would have depended
  on humans for food
47 *bees . . . basin* according to Virgil (et. al.) swarming bees can be attracted by banging a
  metal basin (*Georgics* 4.64)
49 *wax* both noun (what Mammon will produce) and verb – 'to grow [erect]'
  God's gift Dorothea means 'God's gift' in Greek

DOL
What is he, General?

FACE   An *Adalantado*,   50
A grandee, girl. Was not my Dapper here, yet?

DOL
No.

FACE   Nor my Drugger?

DOL   Neither.

FACE   A pox on 'em,
They are so long a-furnishing! Such stinkards
Would not be seen, upon these festival days.

[*Enter* SUBTLE]

How now! Ha' you done?

SUBTLE   Done. They are gone. The sum   55
Is here in bank, my Face. I would, we knew
Another chapman, now, would buy 'em outright.

FACE
'Slid, Nab shall do't, against he ha' the widow,
To furnish household.

SUBTLE   Excellent, well thought on,
Pray God, he come.

FACE   I pray, he keep away   60
Till our new business be o'erpast.

SUBTLE   But, Face,
How camest thou, by this secret Don?

FACE   A spirit
Brought me th' intelligence, in a paper, here,
As I was conjuring, yonder, in my circle
For Surly: I ha' my flies abroad. Your bath   65
Is famous, Subtle, by my means. Sweet Dol,
You must go tune your virginal, no losing
O' the least time. And, do you hear? Good action.
Firk, like a flounder; kiss, like a scallop, close:

53 *a-furnishing* preparing; stocking up
57 *chapman* merchant
62 FACE F2; not inQ, F
69 *Firk, like a flounder* the arching contortions of a flat fish out of water are suggested
     kiss, like a scallop, close editors refer to a Latin poem by the Emperor Gallienus with the
     phrase 'non vincant oscula conchae' ('Don't let a clam's kisses win'). But Jonson
     wouldn't have needed this to remind him of the resemblance between shellfish and female
     genitals which has led many to find shellfish aphrodisiac

And tickle him with thy mother-tongue. His great   70
Verdugoship has not a jot of language:
So much the easier to be cozened, my Dolly.
He will come here, in a hired coach, obscure,
And our own coachman, whom I have sent, as guide,
No creature else.   *One knocks*
        Who's that?
SUBTLE   It i' not he?   75
FACE
  O no, not yet this hour.
SUBTLE   Who is't?
DOL [*At window*]   Dapper,
  Your clerk.
FACE   God's will, then, Queen of Fairy,
  On with your tire; and, Doctor, with your robes.
  Let's despatch him, for God's sake.
SUBTLE   'Twill be long.
FACE
  I warrant you, take but the cues I give you,   80
  It shall be brief enough. 'Slight, here are more!
  Abel, and I think, the angry boy, the heir,
  That fain would quarrel.
SUBTLE   And the widow?
FACE   No,
  Not that I see. Away.   [*Exit* SUBTLE. FACE *opens door*]
      O sir, you are welcome.

Act III, Scene iv

[*Enter*] DAPPER [*to them*]

FACE

The Doctor is within, a-moving for you;

---

70 *mother-tongue* i.e. what lies between the vaginal *labia*
71 *Verdugoship verdugo* is Spanish for 'hangman'
    language English
73 *obscure* concealed
79 *Let's* Lett's vs Q
82 *angry boy* 'angry boys', 'terrible boys' or, most commonly, 'roaring boys' were names
    given to well-heeled thugs

(I have had the most ado to win him to it)
He swears, you'll be the darling o' the dice:
He never heard her Highness dote, till now (he says.)
Your aunt has given you the most gracious words,   5
That can be thought on.

DAPPER   Shall I see her Grace?

FACE

See her, and kiss her, too.

[*Enter* DRUGGER *and* KASTRIL]

What? Honest Nab!
Hast brought the damask?

DRUGGER   No, sir, here's tobacco.

FACE

'Tis well done, Nab: thou'lt bring the damask too?

DRUGGER

Yes, here's the gentleman, Captain, Master Kastril,   10
I have brought to see the Doctor.

FACE   Where's the widow?

DRUGGER

Sir, as he likes, his sister (he says) shall come.

FACE

O, is it so? 'Good time. Is your name Kastril, sir?

KASTRIL

Ay, and the best o' the Kastrils, I'd be sorry else,
By fifteen hundred, a year. Where is this Doctor?   15
My mad tobacco-boy, here, tells me of one,
That can do things. Has he any skill?

FACE   Wherein, sir?

KASTRIL

To carry a business, manage a quarrel, fairly,
Upon fit terms.

FACE   It seems sir, you're but young
About the town, that can make that a question!   20

---

4   (*he says.*) not in Q
8   DRUGGER *Nab* Q, F
9   *Nab* not in Q
18–19   *manage ... terms* quarrelling, like much else, had been systematised and made into a
        science at this period. In *As You Like It* Touchstone goes through the degrees of the lie
        (V.iv.90ff)

KASTRIL

    Sir, not so young, but I have heard some speech
    Of the angry boys, and seen 'em take tobacco;
    And in his shop: and I can take it too.
    And I would fain be one of 'em, and go down
    And practise i' the country.

FACE   Sir, for the *duello*,   25

    The Doctor, I assure you, shall inform you,
    To the least shadow of a hair: and show you,
    An instrument he has, of his own making,
    Wherewith, no sooner shall you make report
    Of any quarrel, but he will take the height on't,   30
    Most instantly; and tell in what degree,
    Of safety it lies in, or mortality.
    And, how it may be borne, whether in a right line,
    Or a half-circle; or may, else, be cast
    Into an angle blunt, if not acute: 35
    All this he will demonstrate. And then, rules,
    To give, and take the lie, by.

KASTRIL   How? To take it?

FACE

    Yes, in oblique, he'll show you; or in circle:
    But never in diameter. The whole town
    Study his theorems, and dispute them, ordinarily,   40
    At the eating academies.

KASTRIL   But, does he teach

    Living, by the wits, too?

FACE   Anything, whatever.

    You cannot think that subtlety, but he reads it.
    He made me a Captain. I was a stark pimp,
    Just o' your standing, 'fore I met with him: 45
    It i' not two months since. I'll tell you his method.
    First, he will enter you, at some ordinary.

---

   25 *duello* duel
   32 *mortality* danger
   39 *in diameter* i.e. head-on; 'the lie direct'
  40–1 *ordinarily . . . academies* Jonson puns on the sense of 'ordinary' as eating house and
      reverses the expected epithets (study and disputation usually take place in academies,
      eating in ordinaries)
   43 *reads* understands
   44 *stark* arrant, unmodified

KASTRIL

No, I'll not come there. You shall pardon me.

FACE   For why, sir?

KASTRIL

There's gaming there, and tricks.

FACE   Why, would you be

A gallant, and not game?

KASTRIL   Ay, 'twill spend a man.   50

FACE

Spend you? It will repair you, when you are spent.

How do they live by their wits, there, that have vented

Six times your fortunes?

KASTRIL   What, three thousand a year!

FACE

Ay, forty thousand.

KASTRIL   Are there such?

FACE   Ay, sir.

And gallants, yet. Here's a young gentleman,   55

Is born to nothing, forty marks a year,

Which I count nothing. He's to be initiated,

And have a fly o' the Doctor. He will win you

By unresistable luck, within this fortnight,

Enough to buy a barony. They will set him   60

Upmost, at the Groom-porter's, all the Christmas!

And, for the whole year through, at every place,

Where there is play, present him with the chair;

The best attendance, the best drink, sometimes

Two glasses of canary, and pay nothing;   65

The purest linen, and the sharpest knife,

The partridge next his trencher: and, somewhere,

The dainty bed, in private, with the dainty.

You shall ha' your ordinaries bid for him,

As playhouses for a poet; and the master   70

Pray him, aloud, to name what dish he affects,

---

50 *spend a man* waste away a man's wealth
58 *fly* see Argument, 1.11
61 *Groom-porter* an officer in the royal household particularly concerned with gaming
    regulations
64 *attendance* service
65 *canary* canary wine
71 *affects* desires

Which must be buttered shrimps: and those that drink
To no mouth else, will drink to his, as being
The goodly, president mouth of all the board.

KASTRIL

Do you not gull one?

FACE   'Od's my life! Do you think it?   75
You shall have a cast commander, (can but get
In credit with a glover, or a spurrier,
For some two pair, of either's ware, aforehand)
Will, by most swift posts, dealing with him,
Arrive at competent means, to keep himself,   80
His punk, and naked boy, in excellent fashion.
And be admired for it.

KASTRIL   Will the Doctor teach this?

FACE

He will do more, sir, when your land is gone,
(As men of spirit hate to keep earth long)
In a vacation, when small money is stirring,   85
And ordinaries suspended till the term,
He'll show a perspective, where on one side
You shall behold the faces, and the persons
Of all sufficient young heirs, in town,
Whose bonds are current for commodity;   90
On th' other side, the merchants' forms, and others,
That, without help of any second broker,
(Who would expect a share) will trust such parcels:
In the third square, the very street, and sign
Where the commodity dwells, and does but wait   95
To be delivered, be it pepper, soap,
Hops, or tobacco, oatmeal, woad, or cheeses.
All which you may so handle, to enjoy,
To your own use, and never stand obliged.

75 *'Od's my life* God's my life Q
76 *cast commander* unemployed officer
77 *spurrier* spur-maker
79 *by most swift posts* with great speed
81 *punk* prostitute, kept woman
    naked boy just that; 'catamite' is the grander term
84 *As men . . . long* this has the logic of a natural law: earth descends, spirit rises
87 *perspective* optical trick
90 *commodity* see II.i.10–14
97 *woad* a blue dye

KASTRIL
  I' faith! Is he such a fellow?
FACE   Why, Nab here knows him.   100
  And then for making matches, for rich widows,
  Young gentlewomen, heirs, the fortunat'st man!
  He's sent to, far, and near, all over England,
  To have his counsel, and to know their fortunes.
KASTRIL
  God's will, my suster shall see him.
FACE   I'll tell you, sir,   105
  What he did tell me of Nab. It's a strange thing!
  (By the way you must eat no cheese, Nab, it breeds melancholy:
  And that same melancholy breeds worms) but pass it –
  He told me, honest Nab, here, was ne'er at tavern,
  But once in's life.
DRUGGER   Truth, and no more I was not.   110
FACE
  And, then he was so sick—
DRUGGER   Could he tell you that, too?
FACE
  How should I know it?
DRUGGER   In troth we had been a-shooting,
  And had a piece of fat ram-mutton, to supper,
  That lay so heavy o' my stomach—
FACE   And he has no head
  To bear any wine; for, what with the noise o' the fiddlers,   115
  And care of his shop, for he dares keep no servants—
DRUGGER
  My head did so ache—
FACE   As he was fain to be brought home,
  The Doctor told me. And then, a good old woman—
DRUGGER
  (Yes, faith, she dwells in Sea-coal Lane) did cure me,
  With sodden ale, and pellitory o' the wall: 120

---

  107 *eat . . . melancholy* milk and its products were thought to engender melancholy. In fact they
       stimulate the production of mucus and, if anything, promote a phlegmatic disposition
  109–26 *He told . . . the Doctor* Face's prompting shows him to know Dapper's story – and its
       wording – by heart
  119 *Sea-coal Lane* now Old Seacoal Lane, running from Farringdon Street to Fleet Lane. It
       was the home of fruiterers
  120 *sodden* boiled

Cost me but two pence. I had another sickness,
Was worse than that.
FACE   Ay, that was with the grief
    Thou took'st for being 'sessed at eighteen pence,
    For the water-work.
DRUGGER   In truth, and it was like
    T'have cost me almost my life.
FACE   Thy hair went off?   125
DRUGGER
    Yes, sir, 'twas done for spite.
FACE   Nay, so says the Doctor.
KASTRIL
    Pray thee, tobacco-boy, go fetch my suster,
    I'll see this learned boy, before I go:
    And so shall she.
FACE   Sir, he is busy now:
    But, if you have a sister to fetch hither,   130
    Perhaps, your own pains may command her sooner;
    And he, by that time, will be free.
KASTRIL   I go.   [*Exit* KASTRIL]
FACE
    Drugger, she's thine: the damask.   [*Exit* DRUGGER]
                            (Subtle, and I
    Must wrestle for her.) Come on, master Dapper.
    You see, how I turn clients, here, away,   135
    To give your cause dispatch. Ha' you performed
    The ceremonies were enjoined you?
DAPPER   Yes, o' the vinegar,
    And the clean shirt.
FACE   'Tis well: that shirt may do you
    More worship than you think. Your aunt's afire,
    But that she will not show it, t'have a sight on you.   140
    Ha' you provided for her Grace's servants?

---

  pellitory o' the wall lichwort (of the same family as stinging nettle and hop); this bushy
  plant which grows in the cracks of walls is used in decoctions and infusions as a remedy
  for urinary disorders
123 *'sessed* assessed (for a rate)
124 *the water-work* see II.i.76. The 'New River', an aqueduct, was under construction at the
  time the play was written
126 *'twas done for spite* i.e. the excessive levy
132 *go* go, Sir Q

DAPPER

Yes, here are six score Edward shillings.

FACE   Good.

DAPPER

And an old Harry's sovereign.

FACE   Very good.

DAPPER

And three James shillings, and an Elizabeth groat,
Just twenty nobles.

FACE   O, you are too just.   145

I would you had had the other noble in Marys.

DAPPER

I have some Philip, and Marys.

FACE   Ay, those same

Are best of all. Where are they? Hark, the Doctor.

Act III, Scene v

[*Enter*] SUBTLE *disguised like a Priest of Fairy* [*to them*]

SUBTLE

Is yet her Grace's cousin come?

FACE   He is come.

SUBTLE

And is he fasting?

FACE   Yes.

SUBTLE   And hath cried *hum*?

FACE

Thrice, you must answer.

---

143 *old Harry's sovereign* a sovereign from the realm of either Henry VII or Henry VIII; worth only 10 shillings
144 *James shillings* i.e. shillings from the present realm
    groat fourpence
145 *nobles* worth 6 shillings and 8 pence
147 *Philip and Marys* these nobles had the heads of the two sovereigns facing each other. Face, true to his name, seems to want his coins to provide a portrait gallery. There was a slight, but insignificant reduction in the fineness of gold coins between the reigns of Mary and James, so Face's enthusiasm for the earlier coins is not based on greed for gold

III.v *H.&S.* cite Edward Marchant's *The seuerall Notorious and lewd Cosenages of Iohn West, and Alice West, falsely called the King and Queen of Fayries.* These two were convicted in 1613 of practices very similar to those described in this scene. Jonson may well have heard of them

DAPPER	Thrice.
SUBTLE	And as oft *buz*?
FACE	

If you have, say.

| DAPPER | I have. |
| SUBTLE | Then, to her coz, |

Hoping, that he hath vinegared his senses,   5
As he was bid, the Fairy Queen dispenses,
By me, this robe, the petticoat of Fortune;
Which that he straight put on, she doth importune.
And though to Fortune near be her petticoat,
Yet, nearer is her smock, the Queen doth note: 10
And, therefore, even of that a piece she hath sent,
Which, being a child, to wrap him in, was rent;
And prays him, for a scarf, he now will wear it
                    They blind him with a rag
(With as much love, as then her Grace did tear it)
About his eyes, to show, he is fortunate.   15
And, trusting unto her to make his state,
He'll throw away all worldly pelf, about him;
Which that he will perform, she doth not doubt him.

FACE

She need not doubt him, sir. Alas, he has nothing,
But what he will part withall, as willingly,   20
Upon her Grace's word (throw away your purse)
                    He throws away, as they bid him
As she would ask it: (handkerchiefs, and all)
She cannot bid that thing, but he'll obey.
(If you have a ring, about you, cast it off,
Or a silver seal, at your wrist, her Grace will send   25
Her fairies here to search you, therefore deal
Directly with her Highness. If they find
That you conceal a mite, you are undone.)

DAPPER

Truly, there's all.

| FACE | All what? |
| DAPPER | My money, truly. |

17 *pelf* property; stuff

FACE

    Keep nothing, that is transitory, about you.   30
    (Bid Dol play music.) Look, the elves are come

              DOL enters with a cithern: they pinch him

    To pinch you, if you tell not truth. Advise you.

DAPPER

    O, I have a paper with a spur-rial in't.

FACE   *Ti, ti,*

    They knew't, they say.

SUBTLE   *Ti, ti, ti, ti,* he has more yet.

FACE

    Ti, ti-ti-ti. I' the tother pocket?

SUBTLE   *Titi, titi, titi, titi.*   35

    They must pinch him, or he will never confess, they say.

DAPPER

    O, O.

FACE   Nay, 'pray you hold. He is her Grace's nephew.
    Ti, ti, ti? What care you? Good faith, you shall care.
    Deal plainly, sir, and shame the fairies. Show
    You are an innocent.

DAPPER   By this good light, I ha' nothing.   40

SUBTLE

    Ti, ti, titi to ta. He does equivocate, she says:
    Ti, ti do ti, ti ti do, ti da. And swears by the light, when
        he is blinded.

DAPPER

    By this good dark, I ha' nothing but a half crown
    Of gold, about my wrist, that my love gave me;
    And a leaden heart I wore, sin' she forsook me.   45

FACE

    I thought, 'twas something. And, would you incur
    Your aunt's displeasure for these trifles? Come,
    I had rather you had thrown away twenty half crowns.
    You may wear your leaden heart still.   [*DOL at window*]
                    How now?

---

32 *cithern* ghittern; an instrument like a guitar
33 *spur-rial* Edward IV noble with a blazing sun on the tail side, resembling the rowel of a spur
41 *equivocate* evade
45 *leaden heart* an emblem of grief

SUBTLE
    What news, Dol?
DOL   Yonder's your knight, sir Mammon.   50
FACE
    God's lid, we never thought of him, till now.
    Where is he?
DOL   Here, hard by. He's at the door.
SUBTLE [*To* FACE]
    And, you are not ready, now? Dol, get his suit.
    He must not be sent back.   [*Exit* DOL]
FACE   O, by no means.
    What shall we do with this same puffin, here,   55
    Now he's o' the spit?
SUBTLE   Why, lay him back a while,
    With some device.

                    [*Enter* DOL]

            Ti, ti ti, ti ti ti. Would her Grace speak
        with me?
    I come. Help, Dol.
                    He speaks through the keyhole, the other knocking
FACE   Who's there? Sir Epicure;
    My master's i' the way. Please you to walk
    Three or four turns, but till his back be turned,   60
    And I am for you. Quickly, Dol.
                    [FACE *dresses as* 'Lungs']
SUBTLE   Her Grace
    Commends her kindly to you, master Dapper.
DAPPER
    I long to see her Grace.
SUBTLE   She, now, is set
    At dinner, in her bed; and she has sent you,
    From her own private trencher, a dead mouse,   65
    And a piece of gingerbread, to be merry withal,
    And stay your stomach, lest you faint with fasting:
    Yet, if you could hold out, till she saw you (she says)
    It would be better for you.

56 *o' the spit* ready for roasting

FACE   Sir, he shall
  Hold out, and 'twere this two hours, for her Highness;   70
  I can assure you that. We will not lose
  All we ha' done—
SUBTLE   He must nor see, nor speak
  To anybody, till then.
FACE   For that, we'll put, sir,
  A stay in 's mouth.
SUBTLE   Of what?
FACE   Of gingerbread.
  Make you it fit. He that hath pleased her Grace,   75
  Thus far, shall not now crinkle, for a little.
  Gape sir, and let him fit you.   [SUBTLE *inserts gag*]
SUBTLE   Where shall we now
  Bestow him?
DOL   I' the privy.
SUBTLE   Come along, sir,
  I now must show you Fortune's privy lodgings.
FACE
  Are they perfumed? And his bath ready?
SUBTLE   All.   80
  Only the fumigation's somewhat strong.
FACE
  Sir Epicure, I am yours, sir, by and by.

          [*Exeunt* SUBTLE, DOL, DAPPER]

Act IV, Scene i

        [*Enter*] MAMMON [*to* FACE]

FACE
  O, sir, you're come i' the only, finest time—
MAMMON
  Where's master?
FACE   Now preparing for projection, sir.
  Your stuff will b' all changed shortly.

74 *stay* gag
76 *crinkle* shrink from his purpose
77 *let him fit you* the term to 'fit' someone could have sinister undertones; e.g. *The Spanish Tragedy*, IV.i.70, 'Why then I'll fit you'
78 *privy* private place; i.e. lavatory

MAMMON   Into gold?

FACE

To gold, and silver, sir.

MAMMON   Silver, I care not for.

FACE

Yes, sir, a little to give beggars.

MAMMON   Where's the lady?   5

FACE

At hand, here. I ha' told her such brave things, o' you,
Touching your bounty and your noble spirit—

MAMMON   Hast thou?

FACE

As she is almost in her fit to see you.
But, good sir, no divinity i' your conference,
For fear of putting her in rage—

MAMMON   I warrant thee.   10

FACE

Six men will not hold her down. And then,
If the old man should hear, or see you—

MAMMON   Fear not.

FACE

The very house, sir, would run mad. You know it
How scrupulous he is, and violent,
'Gainst the least act of sin. Physic, or mathematics,   15
Poetry, state, or bawdry (as I told you)
She will endure, and never startle: but
No word of controversy.

MAMMON   I am schooled, good Ulen.

FACE

And you must praise her house, remember that,
And her nobility.

MAMMON   Let me, alone: 20
No herald, no nor antiquary, Lungs,
Shall do it better. Go.

FACE   (Why, this is yet

---

6   *o'you* on you Q
9   *divinity* theology
16 *state* matters of state; politics
17 *startle* be startled
18 *Ulen* Lungs Q

A kind of modern happiness, to have
Dol Common for a great lady.)   [*Exit* FACE]
MAMMON   Now Epicure,
Heighten thyself, talk to her, all in gold;   25
Rain her as many showers, as Jove did drops
Unto his Danae: show the God a miser,
Compared with Mammon. What? The stone will do't.
She shall feel gold, taste gold, hear gold, sleep gold:
Nay, we will *concumbere* gold. I will be puissant, 30
And mighty in my talk to her! Here she comes.

[*Enter* FACE, DOL]

FACE

To him, Dol, suckle him. This is the noble knight,
I told your ladyship—
MAMMON   Madam, with your pardon,
I kiss your vesture.
DOL   Sir, I were uncivil
If I would suffer that, my lip to you, sir.   35
MAMMON

I hope, my lord your brother be in health, lady?
DOL

My lord, my brother is, though I no lady, sir.
FACE

(Well said my Guinea bird.)
MAMMON   Right noble madam—
FACE

(O, we shall have most fierce idolatry!)
MAMMON

'Tis your prerogative.
DOL   Rather your courtesy. 40
MAMMON

Were there nought else t'enlarge your virtues, to me,
These answers speak your breeding, and your blood.

---

23 *modern* commonplace (and so a play on Dol's name); the sense 'contemporary' was also
  present
26–7 *Rain . . . Danae* see II.i.102
  30 *concumbere* lit. 'lie together' which Mammon seems to use as a transitive verb 'to generate'
   puissant (Fr.) powerful; Mammon perhaps means 'potent'
  38 *Guinea bird* guinea hen and guinea bird were slang terms for prostitute

DOL

Blood we boast none, sir, a poor baron's daughter.

MAMMON

Poor! And gat you? Profane not. Had your father

Slept all the happy remnant of his life   45

After the act, lain but there still, and panted,

He'd done enough, to make himself, his issue,

And his posterity noble.

DOL   Sir, although

We may be said to want the gilt, and trappings,

The dress of honour; yet we strive to keep   50

The seeds, and the materials.

MAMMON   I do see

The old ingredient, virtue, was not lost,

Nor the drug money, used to make your compound.

There is a strange nobility, i' your eye,

This lip, that chin! Methinks you do resemble   55

One o' the Austriac princes.

FACE   (Very like,

Her father was an Irish costermonger.)

MAMMON

The house of Valois, just, had such a nose.

And such a forehead, yet, the Medici

Of Florence boast.

DOL   Troth, and I have been likened   60

To all these princes.

FACE   (I'll be sworn, I heard it.)

MAMMON

I know not how. It is not any one,

But e'en the very choice of all their features.

FACE

(I'll in, and laugh.)   [*Exit* FACE]

MAMMON   A certain touch, or air,

That sparkles a divinity, beyond   65

An earthly beauty!

DOL   O, you play the courtier.

51–3   *The seeds ... compound* Dol and Mammon converse in alchemical metaphors

57   *Irish costermonger* at that time many of the London street vendors were Irish

58–9   *Valois ... Medici* great European houses but not physiognomically marked. Mammon
is name-dropping

MAMMON
　　Good lady, gi' me leave—
DOL　　　　　　　　　　In faith, I may not,
　　To mock me, sir.
MAMMON　　　　To burn i' this sweet flame:
　　The Phoenix never knew a nobler death.
DOL
　　Nay, now you court the courtier: and destroy　　　　70
　　What you would build. This art, sir, i' your words,
　　Calls your whole faith in question.
MAMMON　　　　　　　　By my soul—
DOL
　　Nay, oaths are made o' the same air, sir.
MAMMON　　　　　　　　　　Nature
　　Never bestowed upon mortality,
　　A more unblamed, a more harmonious feature:　　　75
　　She played the stepdame in all faces, else.
　　Sweet madam, le' me be particular—
DOL
　　Particular, sir? I pray you, know your distance.
MAMMON
　　In no ill sense, sweet lady, but to ask
　　How your fair graces pass the hours? I see　　　　80
　　You're lodged, here, i' the house of a rare man,
　　An excellent artist: but, what's that to you?
DOL
　　Yes, sir. I study here the mathematics,
　　And distillation.
MAMMON　　　　O, I cry your pardon.
　　He's a divine instructor! Can extract　　　　　　85
　　The souls of all things, by his art; call all
　　The virtues, and the miracles of the sun,
　　Into a temperate furnace: teach dull nature
　　What her own forces are. A man, the Emperor
　　Has courted, above Kelley: sent his medals,　　　90

69　*Phoenix* a unique and legendary bird that builds its own funeral pyre at regular intervals
　　and, from its own ashes, is born again
70　*court the courtier* use elaborate courtly language
78　*particular* Mammon *could* mean 'let me go into more detail'; but Dol takes 'particular'
　　to mean 'familiar', 'intimate'
90　*Kelley* Edward Kelley (1555–95) who worked with John Dee as his 'scryer'

And chains, t' invite him.
DOL   Ay, and for his physic, sir—
MAMMON
    Above the art of Æsculapius,
    That drew the envy of the Thunderer!
    I know all this, and more.
DOL   Troth, I am taken, sir,
    Whole, with these studies, that contemplate nature.   95
MAMMON
    It is a noble humour. But, this form
    Was not intended to so dark a use!
    Had you been crooked, foul, of some coarse mould,
    A cloister had done well: but, such a feature
    That might stand up the glory of a kingdom,   100
    To live recluse!—is a mere solecism,
    Though in a nunnery. It must not be.
    I muse, my lord your brother will permit it!
    You should spend half my land first, were I he.
    Does not this diamant better, on my finger,   105
    Than i' the quarry?
DOL   Yes.
MAMMON   Why, you are like it.
    You were created, lady, for the light!
    Here, you shall wear it; take it, the first pledge
    Of what I speak: to bind you, to believe me.
DOL
    In chains of adamant?
MAMMON   Yes, the strongest bands.   110
    And take a secret, too. Here, by your side,
    Doth stand, this hour, the happiest man, in Europe.

 91 *chains* these recall the fact that the Emperor Rudolph of Germany imprisoned Kelley
     for failing to produce the Philosopher's Stone
 92 *Æsculapius* son of Apollo and god of medicine. He was able to restore men to life until
     Jupiter ('the Thunderer') killed him with a thunderbolt in order that men should not
     be immortal
96–7; 105–8 compare this specious argument with that used by Milton's Comus to the Lady
     (*Comus*, ll.709–754)
101 *recluse* as a recluse
     solecism error
105 *diamant* diamond
107 *the light* light Q
110 *adamant* puns on 'a diamant'
112 *in* of Q

DOL

You are contented, sir?

MAMMON   Nay, in true being:

The envy of princes, and the fear of states.

DOL

Say you so, Sir Epicure!

MAMMON   Yes, and thou shalt prove it,   115

Daughter of honour. I have cast mine eye

Upon thy form, and I will rear this beauty,

Above all styles.

DOL   You mean no treason, sir!

MAMMON

No, I will take away that jealousy.

I am the lord of the philosopher's stone,   120

And thou the lady.

DOL   How sir! Ha' you that?

MAMMON

I am the master of the mastery.

This day, the good old wretch, here, o' the house

Has made it for us. Now, he's at projection.

Think therefore, thy first wish, now; let me hear it: 125

And it shall rain into thy lap, no shower,

But floods of gold, whole cataracts, a deluge,

To get a nation on thee!

DOL   You are pleased, sir,

To work on the ambition of our sex.

MAMMON

I am pleased, the glory of her sex should know,   130

This nook, here, of the Friars, is no climate

For her, to live obscurely in, to learn

Physic, and surgery, for the Constable's wife

Of some odd Hundred in Essex; but come forth,

And taste the air of places; eat, drink   135

The toils of emp'rics, and their boasted practice;

Tincture of pearl, and coral, gold, and amber;

117–18 *I will rear . . . styles* I will see that this beauty becomes the type of all fashion

122   *mastery* the *magesterium* or master-work

131   *the Friars* Blackfriars

134   *Hundred* a subdivision of a county

136   *The toils of emp'rics* the products of experimental endeavour

Be seen at feasts, and triumphs; have it asked,
What miracle she is? Set all the eyes
Of court afire, like a burning glass,   140
And work 'em into cinders; when the jewels
Of twenty states adorn thee; and the light
Strikes out the stars; that, when thy name is mentioned,
Queens may look pale: and, we but showing our love,
Nero's Poppæa may be lost in story!   145
Thus, will we have it.
DOL   I could well consent, sir.
But, in a monarchy, how will this be?
The Prince will soon take notice; and both seize
You, and your stone: it being a wealth unfit
For any private subject.
MAMMON   If he knew it.   150
DOL
Yourself do boast it, sir.
MAMMON   To thee, my life.
DOL
O, but beware, sir! You may come to end
The remnant of your days, in a loathed prison,
By speaking of it.
MAMMON   'Tis no idle fear!
We'll therefore go with all, my girl, and live   155
In a free state; where we will eat our mullets,
Soused in high-country wines, sup pheasants' eggs,
And have our cockles, boiled in silver shells,
Our shrimps to swim again, as when they lived,
In a rare butter, made of dolphins' milk,   160
Whose cream does look like opals: and, with these
Delicate meats, set ourselves high for pleasure,
And take us down again, and then renew
Our youth, and strength, with drinking the elixir,
And so enjoy a perpetuity   165

---

145 *Nero's Poppæa* so desired by Nero that he had her husband and his own wife killed in
    order to possess her. But she died of a kick from Nero (a typical *lapsus* on Mammon's
    part). Her beauty – and her solicitude for it – were legendary. She is supposed to have
    kept 500 asses in order to be able to bathe daily in their milk *story* history
157 *high-country wines* wines from hill country; but 'high' also suggests their intoxicating effect
160 *rare butter* as Geoffrey Hill remarks, this obvious oxymoron 'is a good, serious joke' (*The
    Lords of Limit*, London, 1984, p. 51)

Of life, and lust. And, thou shalt ha' thy wardrobe,
Richer than Nature's, still, to change thyself,
And vary oftener, for thy pride, than she:
Or Art, her wise, and almost equal servant.

[*Enter* FACE]

FACE

Sir, you are too loud. I hear you, every word,   170
Into the laboratory. Some fitter place.
The garden, or great chamber above. How like you her?

MAMMON

Excellent! Lungs. There's for thee.   [*Gives money*]

FACE   But, do you hear?

Good sir, beware, no mention of the Rabbins.

MAMMON

We think not on 'em.

FACE   O, it is well, sir.   [*Exeunt* DOL, MAMMON]
                                    Subtle!   175

Act IV, Scene ii

[*Enter*] SUBTLE [*to* FACE]

FACE

Dost thou not laugh?

SUBTLE   Yes. Are they gone?

FACE   All's clear.

SUBTLE

The widow is come.

FACE   And your quarrelling disciple?

SUBTLE

Ay.

FACE   I must to my Captainship again, then.

---

166 *lust* both pleasure in general (the German *lust*) and sexual pleasure in particular. It is
     one of the Deadly Sins
167 *Richer than Nature's* see I.iv.27 n.; Shakespeare's Perdita would have considered such an
     attempt to outdo nature overweening and wrong
168 *for thy pride* for your adornment
174 *Rabbins* rabbis; Hugh Broughton, from whose work Dol is to quote copiously, was expert
     in Judaic history and law

SUBTLE
   Stay, bring 'em in, first.
FACE   So I meant. What is she?
   A bonnibell?
SUBTLE   I know not.
FACE   We'll draw lots,   5
   You'll stand to that?
SUBTLE   What else?
FACE   O, for a suit,
   To fall now, like a curtain: flap.
SUBTLE   To th' door, man.
FACE
   You'll ha' the first kiss, 'cause I am not ready.   [*Exit* FACE]
SUBTLE
   Yes, and perhaps hit you through both the nostrils.
FACE [*within*]
   Who would you speak with?
KASTRIL [*within*]   Where's the Captain?
FACE   Gone, sir.   10
   About some business.
KASTRIL   Gone?
FACE   He'll return straight.
   But master Doctor, his lieutenant, is here.

      [*Enter* KASTRIL, DAME PLIANT, *Exit* FACE]

SUBTLE
   Come near, my worshipful boy, my *terrae fili,*
   That is, my boy of land; make thy approaches:
   Welcome, I know thy lusts, and thy desires,   15
   And I will serve, and satisfy 'em. Begin,
   Charge me from thence, or thence, or in this line;
   Here is my centre: ground thy quarrel.
KASTRIL   You lie.

  5 *bonnibell* (Fr.) 'bonne et belle', i.e. a good and pretty woman
  6 *suit* of clothes; Face needs to change into his captain's outfit
  9 *hit . . . nostrils* 'lead you through the nose'
  13 *terrae fili* (Lat.) son of the soil
  17 *charge* accuse; attack
  18 *ground* establish

SUBTLE
    How, child of wrath, and anger! The loud lie?
    For what, my sudden boy?
KASTRIL   Nay, that look you to,   20
    I am aforehand.
SUBTLE   O, this 's no true grammar,
    And as ill logic! You must render causes, child,
    Your first, and second intentions, know your canons,
    And your divisions, moods, degrees, and differences,
    Your predicaments, substance, and accident,   25
    Series extern, and intern, with their causes
    Efficient, material, formal, final,
    And ha' your elements perfect—
KASTRIL   What is this!
    The angry tongue he talks in?
SUBTLE   That false precept,
    Of being aforehand, has deceived a number;   30
    And made 'em enter quarrels, oftentimes,
    Before they were aware: and, afterward,
    Against their wills.
KASTRIL   How must I do then, sir?
SUBTLE
    I cry this lady mercy. She should, first,
    Have been saluted. I do call you lady,   35
    Because you are to be one, ere't be long,

                            He kisses her

    My soft, and buxom widow.
KASTRIL   Is she, i'faith?
SUBTLE
    Yes, or my art is an egregious liar.
KASTRIL
    How know you?
SUBTLE   By inspection, on her forehead,
    And subtlety of her lip, which must be tasted   40

                            He kisses her again

    Often, to make a judgement. 'Slight, she melts

22–8 *You must . . . perfect* Subtle applies the distinctions of logic to the art of quarrelling
  35 *saluted* kissed; greeted

Like a myrobalan! Here is, yet, a line
In *rivo frontis*, tells me, he is no knight.

PLIANT

What is he then, sir?

SUBTLE   Let me see your hand.
O, your *linea Fortunae* makes it plain;   45
And *stella* here, in *monte Veneris*:
But, most of all, *iunctura annularis*.
He is a soldier, or a man of art, lady:
But shall have some great honour, shortly.

PLIANT   Brother,
He's a rare man, believe me!

KASTRIL   Hold your peace.   50

[*Enter* FACE *dressed as Captain*]

Here comes the tother rare man. 'Save you Captain.

FACE

Good master Kastril. Is this your sister?

KASTRIL   Ay, sir.
Please you to kuss her, and be proud to know her?

FACE

I shall be proud to know you, lady.

PLIANT   Brother,
He calls me lady, too.

KASTRIL   Ay, peace. I heard it.   55

[FACE *and* SUBTLE *talk aside*]

FACE

The Count is come.

SUBTLE   Where is he?

FACE   At the door.

SUBTLE

Why, you must entertain him.

FACE   What'll you do
With these the while?

---

42 *myrobalan* fruit, like a plum
43 *in rivo frontis* in the vein of the forehead
45 *linea Fortunae* line of Fortune
46 *stella,,. monte Veneris* star on the mount of Venus (at the base of the thumb)
47 *iunctura annularis* joint of the ring finger
53 *kuss* kiss (Kastril also says 'suster')

SUBTLE   Why, have 'em up, and show 'em
  Some fustian book, or the dark glass.
FACE   'Fore God,
  She is a delicate dab-chick! I must have her.   [*Exit* FACE]   60
SUBTLE
  Must you? Ay, if your fortune will, you must.
  [*To* KASTRIL] Come sir, the Captain will come to us
    presently.
  I'll ha' you to my chamber of demonstrations,
  Where I'll show you both the grammar, and logic,
  And rhetoric of quarrelling; my whole method,   65
  Drawn out in tables; and my instrument,
  That hath the several scale upon't, shall make you
  Able to quarrel, at a straw's breadth, by moonlight.
  And, lady, I'll have you look in a glass,
  Some half an hour, but to clear your eyesight,   70
  Against you see your fortune: which is greater,
  Than I may judge upon the sudden, trust me.
             [*Exeunt* SUBTLE, KASTRIL, PLIANT]

Act IV, Scene iii

[*Enter*] FACE

FACE
  Where are you, Doctor?
SUBTLE [*within*]   I'll come to you presently.
FACE
  I will ha' this same widow, now I ha' seen her,
  On any composition.

[*Enter* SUBTLE]

SUBTLE   What do you say?

---

59 *fustian* written in jargon or cant
   dark glass crystal ball
66 *Drawn out in tables* tabulated
71 *Against* in order that

 3 *composition* deal

FACE

Ha' you disposed of them?

SUBTLE   I ha' sent 'em up.

FACE

Subtle, in troth, I needs must have this widow.   5

SUBTLE

Is that the matter?

FACE   Nay, but hear me.

SUBTLE   Go to,

If you rebel once, Dol shall know it all.

Therefore be quiet, and obey your chance.

FACE

Nay, thou art so violent now – Do but conceive:

Thou art old, and canst not serve—

SUBTLE   Who, cannot I?   10

'Slight, I will serve her with thee, for a—

FACE   Nay,

But understand: I'll gi' you composition.

SUBTLE

I will not treat with thee: what, sell my fortune?

'Tis better than my birthright. Do not murmur.

Win her, and carry her. If you grumble, Dol   15

Knows it directly.

FACE   Well sir, I am silent.

Will you go help, to fetch in Don, in state?   [*Exit* FACE]

SUBTLE

I follow you, sir: we must keep Face in awe,

Or he will overlook us like a tyrant.

[*Enter* FACE,] SURLY *like a Spaniard*

Brain of a tailor! Who comes here? Don John!   20

SURLY

Señores, beso las manos, á vuestras mercedes.

---

10   *serve* a pun on the sense 'inseminate' (which adds a further dimension to 'conceive' in
     the previous line)
11   *'Slight* 'Sblood Q
13   *treat* bargain
19   *overlook* look over; lord it over
20   *Don John* a common type-name for a Spaniard (like Mañuel now)
21   *Senores . . . mercedes* 'Gentlemen, I kiss your worships' hands'

SUBTLE

Would you had stooped a little, and kissed our *anos*.

FACE

Peace Subtle.

SUBTLE   Stab me; I shall never hold, man.

He looks in that deep ruff, like a head in a platter,

Served in by a short cloak upon two trestles!   25

FACE

Or, what do you say to a collar of brawn, cut down

Beneath the souse, and wriggled with a knife?

SUBTLE

'Slud, he does look too fat to be a Spaniard.

FACE

Perhaps some Fleming, or some Hollander got him

In d'Alva's time: Count Egmont's bastard.

SUBTLE   Don,   30

Your scurvy, yellow, Madrid face is welcome.

SURLY

Gratia.

SUBTLE   He speaks, out of a fortification.

Pray God, he ha' no squibs in those deep sets.

SURLY

Por Dios, Señores, muy linda casa!

SUBTLE

What says he?

FACE   Praises the house, I think,   35

I know no more but's action.

24–5 *He looks . . . trestles* cf. John Webster, *The White Devil*, 'He carries his face in's ruff, as I
     have seen a serving-man carry glasses in a cypress hat-band, monstrous steady, for fear
     of breaking' (III.i.75–7)

  27 *souse* ear
     wriggled i.e. the knife has cut a zigzag pattern in the meat so that it looks pleated or
     folded like a ruff

  30 *d'Alva* Fernando Alvarez, Duke of Alva, governor of the Spanish Netherlands between
     1567 and 1573
     Count Egmont a Flemish patriot executed by d'Alva in 1568

  32 *Gratia* thank you

32–3 *He speaks . . . sets* Surly is immured in his ruff and the pleats resemble the crenellations
     of a fortress which could conceal explosives (squibs) in its recesses. The tubular pattern
     of the ruffs' edge would itself evoke gun-barrels pointing outward from embrasures

  34 *Por Dios . . . casa* 'By God gentlemen, a most charming house'

SUBTLE   Yes, the *casa*,
  My precious Diego, will prove fair enough,
  To cozen you in. Do you mark? You shall
  Be cozened, Diego.
FACE   Cozened, do you see?
  My worthy Donzel, cozened.
SURLY   *Entiendo.*   40
SUBTLE
  Do you intend it? So do we, dear Don.
  Have you brought pistolets? Or portagues?

                                    He feels his pockets

  My solemn Don? [*To* FACE] Dost thou feel any?
FACE   [*To* SUBTLE] Full.
SUBTLE
  You shall be emptied, Don; pumped, and drawn,
  Dry, as they say.
FACE   Milked, in troth, sweet Don.   45
SUBTLE
  See all the monsters; the great lion of all, Don.
SURLY
  Con licencia, se puede ver á esta señora?
SUBTLE
  What talks he now?
FACE   O' the *Señora*.
SUBTLE   O, Don,
  That is the lioness, which you shall see
  Also, my Don.
FACE   'Slid, Subtle, how shall we do?   50
SUBTLE
  For what?
FACE   Why, Dol's employed, you know.
SUBTLE   That's true!
  'Fore heaven I know not: he must stay, that's all.
FACE
  Stay? That he must not by no means.

---

40 *Donzel* little Don
    Entiendo I understand
46 *monsters . . . lion* lions were kept in the Tower of London as tourist attractions. Monsters
    (freaks and prodigies of various sorts) were also objects of holiday viewing
47 *Con . . . señora?* 'Is it possible, by your leave, to see the señora?'

SUBTLE   No, why?

FACE

Unless you'll mar all. 'Slight, he'll suspect it.
And then he will not pay, not half so well.   55
This is a travelled punk-master, and does know
All the delays: a notable hot rascal,
And looks, already, rampant.

SUBTLE   'Sdeath, and Mammon
Must not be troubled.

FACE   Mammon, in no case!

SUBTLE

What shall we do then?

FACE   Think: you must be sudden.   60

SURLY

*Entiendo, que la señora es tan hermosa, que codicio tan
á verla, como la bien aventuranza de mi vida.*

FACE

Mi vida? 'Slid, Subtle, he puts me in mind o' the widow.
What dost thou say to draw her to't? Ha?
And tell her, it is her fortune. All our venture   65
Now lies upon 't. It is but one man more,
Which on's chance to have her: and, beside,
There is no maidenhead, to be feared, or lost.
What dost thou think on't, Subtle?

SUBTLE   Who, I? Why—

FACE

The credit of our house too is engaged.   70

SUBTLE

You made me an offer for my share erewhile.
What wilt thou gi' me, i'faith?

FACE   O, by that light,
I'll not buy now. You know your doom to me.
E'en take your lot, obey your chance, sir; win her,
And wear her, out for me.

SUBTLE   'Slight. I'll not work her then.   75

---

60   *sudden* quick
61–2 *Entiendo . . . vida* 'I understand that the señora is so beautiful that I long to see her as if
     she were my life's good fortune'

FACE

    It is the common cause, therefore bethink you.

    Dol else must know it, as you said.

SUBTLE   I care not.

SURLY

    Señores, porqué se tarda tanto?

SUBTLE

    Faith, I am not fit, I am old.

FACE   That's now no reason, sir.

SURLY

    Puede ser, de hacer burla de mi amor?   80

FACE

    You hear the Don, too? By this air, I call.

    And loose the hinges, Dol.

SUBTLE   A plague of hell—

FACE

    Will you then do?

SUBTLE   You're a terrible rogue,

    I'll think of this: will you, sir, call the widow?

FACE

    Yes, and I'll take her too, with all her faults,   85

    Now I do think on't better.

SUBTLE   With all my heart, sir,

    Am I discharged o' the lot?

FACE   As you please.

SUBTLE   Hands.

                         [*They shake hands*]

FACE

    Remember now, that upon any change,

    You never claim her.

SUBTLE   Much good joy, and health to you, sir.

    Marry a whore? Fate, let me wed a witch first.   90

SURLY

    Por estas honradas barbas—

SUBTLE   He swears by his beard.

    Dispatch, and call the brother too.   [*Exit* FACE]

    ‘

78   *Senores . . . tanto?* 'Gentlemen, why so much delay?'

80   *Puede . . . amor* 'Perhaps you are treating my love as a joke?'

82   *loose the hinges* break our bond

91   *Por . . . barbas* 'By this honoured beard . . .'

SURLY   *Tengo dúda Señores,*
    Que no me hágan alguna traición.
SUBTLE
    How, issue on? Yes, *praesto Señor*. Please you
    Enthratha the chambratha, worthy Don;   95
    Where if it please the Fates, in your *bathada*
    You shall be soaked, and stroked, and tubbed, and rubbed:
    And scrubbed, and fubbed, dear Don, before you go.
    You shall, in faith, my scurvy baboon Don:
    Be curried, clawed, and flawed, and tawed, indeed.   100
    I will the heartilier go about it now,
    And make the widow a punk, so much the sooner,
    To be revenged on this impetuous Face:
    The quickly doing of it is the grace.

                                   [*Exeunt* SUBTLE, SURLY]

Act IV, Scene iv

[*Enter*] FACE, KASTRIL, DAME PLIANT

FACE
    Come lady: I knew, the Doctor would not leave,
    Till he had found the very nick of her fortune.
KASTRIL
    To be a Countess, say you?
FACE   A Spanish Countess, sir.
PLIANT
    Why? Is that better than an English countess?
FACE
    Better? 'Slight, make you that a question, lady?   5
KASTRIL
    Nay, she is a fool, Captain, you must pardon her.

92–3 *Tengo . . . traición* 'I suspect, gentlemen, that you are practising some kind of treachery
        on me'
 100 *curried* tickled; rubbed down (as in 'curry comb')
        flawed flayed
        tawed beaten (like leather being made pliable for use)

   2 *nick* hiding place
   3 FACE Q; not in F

FACE
>   Ask from your courtier, to your Inns of Court-man,
>   To your mere milliner: they will tell you all,
>   Your Spanish jennet is the best horse. Your Spanish
>   Stoop is the best garb. Your Spanish beard   10
>   Is the best cut. Your Spanish ruffs are the best
>   Wear. Your Spanish pavan the best dance.
>   Your Spanish titillation in a glove
>   The best perfume. And, for your Spanish pike,
>   And Spanish blade, let your poor Captain speak.   15
>   Here comes the Doctor.

[*Enter* SUBTLE]

SUBTLE   My most honoured lady,
>   (For so I am now to style you, having found
>   By this my scheme, you are to undergo
>   All honourable fortune, very shortly.)
>   What will you say now, if some—

FACE   I ha' told her all, sir.   20
>   And her right worshipful brother, here, that she shall be
>   A Countess: do not delay 'em, sir. A Spanish Countess.

SUBTLE
>   Still, my scarce worshipful Captain, you can keep
>   No secret. Well, since he has told you, madame,
>   Do you forgive him, and I do.

KASTRIL   She shall do that, sir.   25
>   I'll look to't, 'tis my charge.

SUBTLE   Well then. Nought rests
>   But that she fit her love, now, to her fortune.

PLIANT
>   Truly, I shall never brook a Spaniard.

SUBTLE   No?

---

   9 *jennet* small Spanish horse
 10 *Stoop* bow
 12 *pavan* a stately dance, introduced into England in the 16th century
 13 *titillation* means of titillating – in this case scent
14–15 *pike . . . blade* Toledo is still famous for its steel. The vogue for things Spanish at court
       was due to James' desire for a closer link with Spain
 18 *scheme* planetary chart
     undergo there is a sexual innuendo here

[137]

PLIANT
 Never, sin' eighty-eight could I abide 'em,
 And that was some three year afore I was born, in truth. 30
SUBTLE
 Come, you must love him, or be miserable:
 Choose, which you will.
FACE   By this good rush, persuade her,
 She will cry strawberries else, within this twelvemonth.
SUBTLE
 Nay, shads, and mackerel, which is worse.
FACE   Indeed, sir?
KASTRIL
 God's lid, you shall love him, or I'll kick you.
PLIANT   Why? 35
 I'll do as you will ha' me, brother.
KASTRIL   Do,
 Or by this hand, I'll maul you.
FACE   Nay, good sir,
 Be not so fierce.
SUBTLE   No, my enraged child,
 She will be ruled. What, when she comes to taste
 The pleasure of a Countess! To be courted— 40
FACE
 And kissed, and ruffled!
SUBTLE   Ay, behind the hangings.
FACE
 And then come forth in pomp!
SUBTLE   And know her state!
FACE
 Of keeping all th'idolators o' the chamber
 Barer to her, than at their prayers!

---

29 *eighty-eight* 1588, the year of the Armada. Dame Pliant's voice is typical of popular
  anti-Spanish sentiment of the time
30 which makes Dame Pliant nineteen
32 *rush* rushes were used as floor cover in houses and on theatre stages
33 *cry strawberries* become a street fruit vendor
34 *shads* a species of herring; Subtle suggests that it is worse to sell fish than fruit. 'Fish wife'
  is still a derogatory term
41 *behind the hangings* wall-hangings – like the arras in *Hamlet* – provided useful hiding-
  places in great houses
44 *Barer* of their hats (and perhaps more)

SUBTLE   Is served

   Upon the knee!

FACE   And has her pages, ushers,   45

   Footmen, and coaches—

SUBTLE   Her six mares—

FACE   Nay, eight!

SUBTLE

   To hurry her through London, to th' Exchange,

   Bedlam, the China-houses—

FACE   Yes, and have

   The citizens gape at her, and praise her tires!

   And my lord's goose-turd bands, that rides with her!   50

KASTRIL

   Most brave! By this hand, you are not my suster,

   If you refuse.

PLIANT   I will not refuse, brother.

                 [*Enter* SURLY]

SURLY

   Qué es esto, Señores, que no se venga?

   Esta tardanza me mata!

FACE   It is the Count come!

   The Doctor knew he would be here, by his art.   55

SUBTLE

   En galanta madama, Don! Galantissima!

SURLY

   Por todos los dioses, la más acabada

   Hermosura, que he visto en mi vida!

FACE

   Is't not a gallant language, that they speak?

---

47 *th' Exchange* the New Exchange in the Strand – a fashionable meeting place where
    negotiations and purchases took place. It was opened in 1609

48 *Bedlam* Bethlehem Royal Hospital for the insane. Viewing the inmates was considered
    a chic pastime
    China-houses London shops where Oriental silks and porcelains were sold. These three
    places are also found grouped together as loci for fashionable living in *Epicoene*,
    IV.iii.24–5

49 *tires* attires

50 *goose-turd bands* collars of the fashionable goose-turd shade of green

53–4 *Qué . . . mata* 'Why doesn't she come, gentlemen? This delay is killing me'

56 *En . . . Galantissima!* Subtle speaks a made-up Spanglish: 'A fine woman, Don, very fine!'

57–8 *Por . . . vida!* 'By all the gods, the most perfect beauty that I have seen in [all] my life!'

KASTRIL
An admirable language! Is't not French?

FACE
No, Spanish, sir.

KASTRIL   It goes like law-French,   60
And that, they say, is the courtliest language.

FACE   List, sir.

SURLY
El sol ha perdido su lumbre, con el
Resplandor, que trae esta dama. Válgame dios!

FACE
He admires your sister.

KASTRIL   Must not she make curtsey?   65

SUBTLE
'Ods will, she must go to him, man; and kiss him!
It is the Spanish fashion, for the women
To make first court.

FACE   'Tis true he tells you, sir:
His art knows all.

SURLY   *Porqué no se acude?*

KASTRIL
He speaks to her, I think?

FACE   That he does sir.   70

SURLY
Por el amor de dios, qué es esto, que se tarda?

KASTRIL
Nay, see: she will not understand him! Gull.
Noddy.

PLIANT   What say you brother?

KASTRIL   Ass, my suster,
Go kuss him, as the cunning man would ha' you, ,
I'll thrust a pin i' your buttocks else.

FACE   O, no sir.   75

---

61   *law-French* a very corrupt derivation of Norman French, still used in law-courts at the date of the play though discontinued soon after

62   *courtliest* in this case the language of the law courts rather than the royal court
     List listen

63–4   *El ... Dios!* 'The sun has lost its light with the splendour that this lady bears, so help me God!'

69   *Porqué ... acude?* 'Why doesn't she come?'

71   *Por ... tarda?* 'For the love of God, what is it that makes her delay?'

SURLY
Señora mía, mi persona muy indigna está
Á llegar á tanta hermosura.

FACE
Does he not use her bravely?

KASTRIL   Bravely, i' faith!

FACE
Nay, he will use her better.

KASTRIL   Do you think so?

SURLY
Señora, si sera servida, entremos.   80

                  [*Exeunt* SURLY, DAME PLIANT]

KASTRIL
Where does he carry her?

FACE   Into the garden, sir;
Take you no thought: I must interpret for her.

SUBTLE
Give Dol the word   [*Exit* FACE]
Come, my fierce child, advance,
We'll to our quarrelling lesson again.

KASTRIL   Agreed.
I love a Spanish boy, with all my heart.   85

SUBTLE
Nay, and by this means, sir, you shall be brother
To a great Count.

KASTRIL   Ay, I knew that, at first.
This match will advance the house of the Kastrils.

SUBTLE
Pray God, your sister prove but pliant.

KASTRIL   Why,
Her name is so: by her other husband.

SUBTLE   How!   90

KASTRIL
The widow Pliant. Knew you not that?

76–7 *Señora . . . hermosura* 'My lady, my person is wholly unworthy to approach such beauty'
  80 *Señora . . . entremos* 'Señora, if it is convenient, let us go in.' (There is a pun on 'serve' here)
  83 *the word* i.e. to begin her 'fit'
  87 *great Count* an aural quibble on 'cunt'

SUBTLE   No faith, sir.
  Yet, by erection of her figure, I guessed it.
  Come, let's go practise.
KASTRIL   Yes, but do you think, Doctor,
  I e'er shall quarrel well?
SUBTLE   I warrant you.

                              [*Exeunt* SUBTLE, KASTRIL]

Act IV, Scene v

          [*Enter*] DOL *in her fit of talking,* MAMMON

DOL
  For, after Alexander's death—
MAMMON   Good lady—
DOL
  That Perdiccas, and Antigonus were slain,
  The two that stood, Seleuc', and Ptolomee—
MAMMON
  Madam.
DOL   Made up the two legs, and the fourth Beast.
  That was Gog-north, and Egypt-south: which after   5
  Was called Gog-Iron-leg, and South-Iron-leg—
MAMMON   Lady—
DOL
  And then Gog-horned. So was Egypt, too.
  Then Egypt-clay-leg, and Gog-clay-leg—
MAMMON   Sweet madam.
DOL
  And last God-dust, and Egypt-dust, which fall

92   *by erection of her figure* by the drawing of her horoscope. Subtle also suggests the erection
      which Dame Pliant's figure has aroused in him

1–32   *after . . . Rome* Dol's diatribe is a patchwork of quotations from Hugh Broughton's *A Concent
        of Scripture* (1590) which attempts to answer questions of Old Testament chronology
  2–3   *Perdicas . . . Antigonus . . . Seleuc' . . . Ptolomee* the four generals of Alexander the Great,
        recipients of his divided empire. Alexander's empire was interpreted as one of the 'four
        kingdoms' mentioned by Daniel in his interpretation of Nebuchadnezzar's dream

In the last link of the fourth chain. And these   10
Be stars in story, which none see, or look at—

MAMMON

What shall I do?

DOL   For, as he says, except
We call the Rabbins, and the heathen Greeks—

MAMMON

Dear lady.

DOL   To come from Salem, and from Athens,
And teach the people of Great Britain—

[Enter FACE *dressed as bellows-man]*

FACE   What's the matter, sir?   15

DOL

To speak the tongue of Eber, and Javan—

MAMMON   O,
She's in her fit.

DOL   We shall know nothing—

FACE   Death, sir,
We are undone.

DOL   Where, then, a learned linguist
Shall see the ancient used communion
Of vowels, and consonants—

FACE   My master will hear!   20

DOL

A wisdom, which Pythagoras held most high—

MAMMON

Sweet honourable lady.

DOL   To comprise
All sounds of voices, in few marks of letters—

FACE

Nay, you must never hope to lay her now.

They speak together

---

10 *the fourth chain* 'Fiue, as it were, chaines of time are in Scripture . . . the fourth chaine
    containeth the continuance of Nebuchadnezar's 70 yeares', Broughton, *Daniel his Chaldie
    Visions and his Ebrew*, London, 1596, Hijv
14 *Salem* Jerusalem
16 *Eber, and Javan* Hebrew and Gentile tongues

DOL

And so we may arrive by
                    Talmud skill,
And profane Greek, to

    raise the building up
Of Helen's house, against

        the Ismaelite,
King of Thogarma, and

        his habergeons
Brimstony, blue, and

        fiery; and the force
Of King Abaddon, and

        the Beast of Cittim:
Which Rabbi David

        Kimchi, Onkelos,
And Aben-Ezra do

    interpret Rome.

FACE

How did you put her
into't?
MAMMON   Alas I talked   25
Of a fifth monarchy I
                would erect,
With the philosopher's
stone (by chance) and she
Falls on the other four,
straight.   FACE Out of
                Broughton!
I told you so. 'Slid stop
her mouth.   MAMMON Is't
                best?

FACE

She'll never leave else.
If the old man hear her,   30
We are but fæces, ashes.
SUBTLE [*within*] What's to
                do there?

FACE

O, we are lost. Now she
hears him, she is quiet.

Upon SUBTLE's *entry they disperse*
                    [*Exeunt* DOL *and* FACE]

MAMMON

Where shall I hide me?
SUBTLE   How! What sight is here!
Close deeds of darkness, and that shun the light!
Bring him again. Who is he? What, my son!   35
O, I have lived too long.
MAMMON   Nay good, dear Father,
There was no unchaste purpose.

---

25   *Talmud* the great rabbinical thesaurus
25,29   MAMMON MAN. F
  26   *fifth monarchy* the millennium; identified with the 'stone ... cut out of the mountain
      without hands ... that ... brake in pieces the iron, the brass, the clay, the silver and the
      gold' of *Daniel* ii.45 – the fifth kingdom which will destroy the other four imaged by the
      clay-footed statue of Nebuchadnezzar's dream
  27   *With the* Which the Q

SUBTLE   Not? And flee me,
    When I come in?
MAMMON   That was my error.
SUBTLE   Error?
    Guilt, guilt, my son. Give it the right name. No marvel,
    If I found check in our great work within,   40
    When such affairs as these were managing!
MAMMON
    Why, have you so?
SUBTLE   It has stood still this half hour:
    And all the rest of our less works gone back.
    Where is the instrument of wickedness,
    My lewd false drudge?
MAMMON   Nay, good sir, blame not him   45
    Believe me, 'twas against his will, or knowledge.
    I saw her by chance.
SUBTLE   Will you commit more sin,
    T'excuse a varlet?
MAMMON   By my hope, 'tis true, sir.
SUBTLE
    Nay, then I wonder less, if you, for whom
    The blessing was prepared, would so tempt heaven: 50
    And lose your fortunes.
MAMMON   Why, sir?
SUBTLE   This'll retard
    The work, a month at least.
MAMMON   Why, if it do,
    What remedy? But think it not, good Father:
    Our purposes were honest.
SUBTLE   As they were,
    So the reward will prove.
                        A great crack and noise within
                        How now! Ay me.   55
    God, and all saints be good to us. What's that?

41 *managing* taking place
42 *stood still* gone back Q
43 *gone back* stand still Q
51 *This'll retard* This will hinder Q

[*Enter* FACE]

FACE

O sir, we are defeated! All the works
Are flown *in fumo*: every glass is burst.
Furnace, and all rent down! As if a bolt
Of thunder had been driven through the house.   60
Retorts, receivers, pelicans, boltheads,
All struck in shivers!

SUBTLE *falls down as in a swoon*

Help, good, sir! Alas,
Coldness, and death invades him. Nay, sir Mammon,
Do the fair offices of a man! You stand,
As you were readier to depart, than he.   65

One knocks

Who's there? My lord her brother is come.

MAMMON   Ha, Lungs?

FACE

His coach is at the door. Avoid his sight,
For he's as furious, as his sister is mad.

MAMMON

Alas!

FACE   My brain is quite undone with the fume, sir,
I ne'er must hope to be mine own man again.   70

MAMMON

Is all lost, Lungs? Will nothing be preserved,
Of all our cost?

FACE   Faith, very little, sir.
A peck of coals, or so, which is cold comfort, sir.

MAMMON

O my voluptuous mind! I am justly punished.

FACE

And so am I, sir.

MAMMON   Cast from all my hopes —   75

FACE

Nay, certainties, sir.

---

58 *in fumo* in smoke
61 *receivers* vessels used to retain distillates

MAMMON   By mine own base affections.
                        SUBTLE *seems to come to himself*

SUBTLE
   O, the curst fruits of vice, and lust!
MAMMON   Good father,
   It was my sin. Forgive it.
SUBTLE   Hangs my roof
   Over us still, and will not fall, O justice,
   Upon us, for this wicked man!
FACE   Nay, look, sir,   80
   You grieve him, now, with staying in his sight:
   Good sir, the nobleman will come too, and take you,
   And that may breed a tragedy.
MAMMON   I'll go.
FACE
   Ay, and repent at home, sir. It may be,
   For some good penance, you may ha' it, yet,   85
   A hundred pound to the box at Bedlam—
MAMMON   Yes.
FACE
   For the restoring such as ha' their wits.
MAMMON   I'll do't.
FACE
   I'll send one to you to receive it.
MAMMON   Do.
   Is no projection left?
FACE   All flown, or stinks, sir.
MAMMON
   Will nought be saved, that's good for med'cine, thinkst thou?   90
FACE
   I cannot tell, sir. There will be, perhaps,
   Something, about the scraping of the shards,
   Will cure the itch: though not your itch of mind, sir.
   It shall be saved for you, and sent home. Good sir,
   This way: for fear the lord should meet you.
                                          [*Exit* MAMMON]

86   *box* charity collection box
93   *itch* a contagious pustular disease in which the skin is inflamed and itchy

SUBTLE   Face.   95

FACE

  Ay.

SUBTLE Is he gone?

FACE   Yes, and as heavily

  As all the gold he hoped for, were in his blood.

  Let us be light, though.

SUBTLE   Ay, as balls, and bound

  And hit our heads against the roof for joy:

  There's so much of our care now cast away.   100

FACE

  Now to our Don.

SUBTLE   Yes, your young widow, by this time

  Is made a Countess, Face: she's been in travail

  Of a young heir for you.

FACE   Good, sir.

SUBTLE   Off with your case,

  And greet her kindly, as a bridegroom should,

  After these common hazards.

FACE   Very well, sir.   105

  Will you go fetch Don Diego off, the while?

SUBTLE

  And fetch him over too, if you'll be pleased, sir:

  Would Dol were in her place, to pick his pockets now.

FACE

  Why, you can do it as well, if you would set to't.

  I pray you prove your virtue.

SUBTLE   For your sake, sir.   110

                    [*Exeunt* SUBTLE *and* FACE]

---

  98 *balls* bubbles

99–100 the final syllables of these lines would have rhymed in 17th-century pronunciation

  102 *travail* labour

  103 *case* disguise

  106 *fetch . . . off* keep him away

  107 *fetch . . . over* get one up on him

Act IV, Scene vi

[*Enter*] SURLY, DAME PLIANT

SURLY
Lady, you see into what hands you are fall'n;
'Mongst what a nest of villians! And how near
Your honour was t'have catched a certain clap
(Through your credulity) had I but been
So punctually forward, as place, time,   5
And other circumstance would ha' made a man:
For you're a handsome woman: would y'were wise, too.
I am a gentleman, come here disguised,
Only to find the knaveries of this citadel,
And where I might have wronged your honour, and have not,   10
I claim some interest in your love. You are,
They say, a widow, rich: and I am a bachelor,
Worth nought: your fortunes may make me a man,
As mine ha' preserved you a woman. Think upon it,
And whether, I have deserved you, or no.
PLIANT   I will, sir.   15
SURLY
And for these household-rogues, let me alone,
To treat with them.

[*Enter* SUBTLE]

SUBTLE   How doth my noble Diego?
And my dear madam, Countess? Hath the Count
Been courteous, lady? Liberal? And open?
Donzell, methinks you look melancholic,   20
After your *coitum*, and scurvy! Truly,
I do not like the dulness of your eye:
It hath a heavy cast, 'tis upsee Dutch,
And says you are a lumpish whore-master,
Be lighter, I will make your pockets so.   25
                    He falls to picking of them

---

3   *clap* then, as now, gonorrhoea; but also used to mean any sudden stroke of misfortune
16 SURLY SVB. F
23 *upsee Dutch* from the Dutch *op zijn*: 'to be up'; i.e. a drinking term like 'bottoms up';
    here the phrase probably means something like 'drunk as a Dutchman'

SURLY

Will you, Don bawd, and pickpurse? How now?

                        [*Sets on him*]
                Reel you?

Stand up sir, you shall find since I am so heavy,
I'll gi' you equal weight.

SUBTLE   Help, murder!

SURLY   No, sir.

There's no such thing intended. A good cart,
And a clean whip shall ease you of that fear.   30
I am the Spanish Don, that should be cozened,
Do you see? Cozened? Where's your Captain Face?
That parcel-broker, and whole-bawd, all rascal.

         [*Enter* FACE *dressed as Captain*]

FACE

How, Surly!

SURLY   O, make your approach, good Captain.

I have found, from whence your copper rings, and spoons   35
Come now, wherewith you cheat abroad in taverns.
'Twas here, you learned t'anoint your boot with brimstone,
Then rub men's gold on't, for a kind of touch,
And say 'twas naught, when you had changed the colour,
That you might ha't for nothing? And this Doctor,   40
Your sooty, smoky-bearded compeer, he
Will close you so much gold, in a bolt's head,
And, on a turn, convey (i' the stead) another
With sublimed mercury, that shall burst i' the heat,
And fly out all *in fumo*? Then weeps Mammon: 45
Then swoons his worship. Or, he is the Faustus,

                      [FACE *slips out*]

29–30   *cart . . . whip* to be whipped behind a cart was a common public punishment for prostitutes
   33   *parcel-broker* part-broker; 'broker' means 'pawnbroker'; probably a receiver of stolen goods
37–9   *anoint . . . colour* gold was tested by being rubbed against touchstone on which it left a
        trace whose quality could be analysed
40–5   *Doctor . . . in fumo* a trick by which the fraudulent alchemist pockets the gold (in a bolt's
        head) and replaces it with a similar container holding mercury which will then explode
        and give the appearance of the gold being lost in smoke
   41   *compeer* colleague
   46   *Faustus* Johann Faustus, the damned necromancer hero of Marlowe's *Doctor Faustus*

That casteth figures, and can conjure, cures
Plague, piles, and pox, by the ephemerides,
And holds intelligence with all the bawds,
And midwives of three shires? While you send in—　　　　50
Captain, (what is he gone?) damsels with child,
Wives, that are barren, or, the waiting-maid
With the green sickness?　　　　　[SUBTLE *attempts to leave*]
　　　　　　　　　　Nay, sir, you must tarry
Though he be 'scaped; and answer, by the ears, sir.

Act IV, Scene vii

[*Enter*] FACE, KASTRIL [*to them*]

FACE
Why, now's the time, if ever you will quarrel
Well (as they say) and be a true-born child.
The Doctor, and your sister both are abused.
KASTRIL
Where is he? Which is he? He is a slave
Whate'er he is, and the son of a whore. Are you　　　　5
The man, sir, I would know?
SURLY　　　　　　　　　　I should be loath, sir,
To confess so much.
KASTRIL　　　　　　　Then you lie, i' your throat.
SURLY　　　　　　　　　　　　　　How?
FACE
A very errant rogue, sir, and a cheater,
Employed here, by another conjurer,
That does not love the Doctor, and would cross him　　　　10
If he knew how—
SURLY　　　　　Sir, you are abused.
KASTRIL　　　　　　　　　　You lie:
And 'tis no matter.
FACE　　　　　　Well said, sir. He is
The impudentest rascal—

48　*ephemerides* an almanac indicating planetary positions for astrological use
53　*green sickness* an anaemic disease to which pubertal women are susceptible
54　*by the ears* see I.i.169

2　*child* the sense 'nobly born' was still current

SURLY   You are indeed. Will you hear me, sir?
FACE
   By no means: bid him be gone.
KASTRIL   Be gone, sir, quickly.
SURLY
   This's strange! Lady, do you inform your brother.   15
FACE
   There is not such a foist, in all the town,
   The Doctor had him, presently: and finds, yet,
   The Spanish Count will come, here. Bear up, Subtle.
SUBTLE
   Yes, sir, he must appear, within this hour.
FACE
   And yet this rogue, would come, in a disguise,   20
   By the temptation of another spirit,
   To trouble our art, though he could not hurt it.
KASTRIL   Ay,
   I know – Away, you talk like a foolish mauther.

                              [*Exit* DAME PLIANT]

SURLY
   Sir, all is truth, she says.
FACE   Do not believe him, sir:
   He is the lyingest swabber! Come your ways, sir.   25
SURLY
   You are valiant, out of company.
KASTRIL   Yes, how then, sir?

                         [*Enter* DRUGGER]

   Nay, here's an honest fellow too, that knows him,
   And all his tricks. (Make good what I say, Abel,)
   This cheater would ha' cozened thee o' the widow.
   He owes this honest Drugger, here, seven pound,   30
   He has had on him, in two-penny 'orths of tobacco.
DRUGGER
   Yes sir. And he's damned himself, three terms, to pay me.

   16 *foist* cheat, rogue
   23 *mauther* young woman
   25 *swabber* deck-hand
   26 *out of* 'because you are in'
   32 *he's* he hath Q

                              [152]

FACE
  And what does he owe for *lotium?*
DRUGGER   Thirty shillings, sir:
  And for six syringes.
SURLY   Hydra of villany!
FACE
  Nay, sir, you must quarrel him out o' the house.
KASTRIL   I will.   35
  Sir, if you get not out o' doors, you lie:
  And you are a pimp.
SURLY   Why, this is madness, sir,
  Not valour in you: I must laugh at this.
KASTRIL
  It is my humour: you are a pimp, and a trig,
  And an Amadis de Gaul, or a Don Quixote.   40
DRUGGER
  Or a Knight o' the Curious Coxcomb. Do you see?

               [*Enter* ANANIAS]

ANANIAS
  Peace to the household.
KASTRIL   I'll keep peace, for no man.
ANANIAS
  Casting of dollars is concluded lawful.
KASTRIL
  Is he the Constable?
SUBTLE   Peace, Ananias.
FACE   No, sir.
KASTRIL
  Then you are an otter, and a shad, a whit,   45
  A very tim.

  33 *lotium* stale urine used by barbers as a lye for the hair
  34 *Hydra* a monster whose many heads multiplied each time one was severed – a fitting
      epithet for Face
  39 *trig* coxcomb
  40 *Amadis de Gaul* the name of a Spanish or Portuguese romance written up by Garcia de
      Montalvo in the second half of the 15th century
      Don Quixote eponymous hero of Cervantes' novel; the *Amadis de Gaul* is one of the few
      romances excused from burning in *Don Quixote*
  41 *Knight o' the Curious Coxcomb* a reference to Surly's extraordinary headgear
  45–6 *shad . . . whit . . . tim* the first of these is a small fish; the *OED* cites this passage in defining
      the other two as terms of abuse; they are Kastril's homemade insults; each has a diminutive
      sound

SURLY   You'll hear me, sir?
KASTRIL   I will not.
ANANIAS
  What is the motive?
SURLY   Zeal, in the young gentleman,
  Against his Spanish slops—
ANANIAS   They are profane,
  Lewd, superstitious, and idolatrous breeches.
SURLY
  New rascals!
KASTRIL   Will you be gone, sir?
ANANIAS   Avoid Satan,   50
  Thou art not of the light. That ruff of pride,
  About thy neck, betrays thee: and is the same
  With that, which the unclean birds, in seventy-sevean,
  Were seen to prank it with, on divers coasts.
  Thou look'st like Antichrist, in that lewd hat.   55
SURLY
  I must give way.
KASTRIL   Be gone, sir.
SURLY   But I'll take
  A course with you—
ANANIAS   (Depart, proud Spanish fiend)
SURLY
  Captain, and Doctor—
ANANIAS   Child of perdition.
KASTRIL   Hence, sir.
                                   [*Exit* SURLY]
  Did I not quarrel bravely?
FACE   Yes, indeed, sir.
KASTRIL
  Nay, and I give my mind to't, I shall do't.   60
FACE
  O, you must follow, sir, and threaten him tame.
  He'll turn again else.
KASTRIL   I'll re-turn him, then.   [*Exit* KASTRIL]

52–4 *the same . . . coasts* Malcolm H. South argues that the 'unclean birds' are Catholic seminary
  priests trained on the Continent and returned to England wearing outlandish ruffs. 'The
  Vncleane Birds, in Seuenty-Seven: *The Alchemist' Studies in English Literature 1500–1900*,
  xiii (1973), pp. 331–43

FACE

    Drugger, this rogue prevented us, for thee:

    We had determined, that thou shouldst ha' come,

    In a Spanish suit, and ha' carried her so; and he　　　　　　65

    A brokerly slave, goes, puts it on himself.

    Hast brought the damask?

DRUGGER　　　　　　　　　　　Yes sir.

FACE　　　　　　　　　　　　　　　　　Thou must borrow,

    A Spanish suit. Hast thou no credit with the players?

DRUGGER

    Yes, sir, did you never see me play the fool?

FACE

    I know not, Nab: thou shalt, if I can help it.　　　　　　70

    Hieronymo's old cloak, ruff, and hat will serve,

    I'll tell thee more, when thou bring'st 'em.　　　[*Exit* DRUGGER]

                SUBTLE *hath whispered with him this while*

ANANIAS　　　　　　　　　　　　　Sir, I know

    The Spaniard hates the Brethren, and hath spies

    Upon their actions: and that this was one

    I make no scruple. But the holy Synod　　　　　　　　75

    Have been in prayer, and meditation, for it.

    And 'tis revealed no less, to them, than me,

    That casting of money is most lawful.

SUBTLE　　　　　　　　　　　　　True.

    But here, I cannot do it; if the house

    Should chance to be suspected, all would out,　　　　80

    And we be locked up, in the Tower, forever,

    To make gold there (for th' state) never come out:

    And, then, are you defeated.

ANANIAS　　　　　　　　　　I will tell

    This to the Elders, and the weaker Brethren,

  63　*prevented* forestalled

67–8　*borrow . . . players* stage costumes were augmented by court cast-offs so actors might
    have a supply of the Spanish clothes in fashion at Court

  69　*did you never see me play the fool?* an illusion-breaking joke: the part of Drugger would have
    been taken by the leading comic actor in the company – Robert Armin in the first instance

  71　*Hieronymo* the crazed, revenging hero of Kyd's *Spanish Tragedy*. It is possible that Jonson
    played this role

That the whole company of the Separation   85
May join in humble prayer again.
SUBTLE   (And fasting.)
ANANIAS
Yea, for some fitter place. The peace of mind
Rest with these walls.
SUBTLE   Thanks, courteous Ananias.

[*Exit* ANANIAS]

FACE
What did he come for?
SUBTLE   About casting dollars,
Presently, out of hand. And so, I told him,   90
A Spanish minister came here to spy,
Against the faithful—
FACE   I conceive. Come Subtle,
Thou art so down upon the least disaster!
How wouldst th' ha' done, if I had not helped thee out?
SUBTLE
I thank thee Face, for the angry boy, i' faith.   95
FACE
Who would ha' looked, it should ha' been that rascal?
Surly? He had dyed his beard, and all. Well, sir,
Here's damask come, to make you a suit.
SUBTLE   Where's Drugger?
FACE
He is gone to borrow me a Spanish habit,
I'll be the Count, now.
SUBTLE   But where's the widow?   100
FACE
Within, with my lord's sister: Madam Dol
Is entertaining her.
SUBTLE   By your favour, Face,
Now she is honest, I will stand again.
FACE
You will not offer it?
SUBTLE   Why?
FACE   Stand to your word,
Or—here comes Dol. She knows—

96   *looked* realised; thought
104   SUBTLE SVR. F

SUBTLE   You're tyrannous still.   105

[*Enter* DOL]

FACE
  Strict for my right. How now, Dol? Hast told her,
  The Spanish Count will come?
DOL   Yes, but another is come,
  You little looked for!
FACE   Who's that?
DOL   Your master:
  The master of the house.
SUBTLE   How, Dol!
FACE   She lies.
  This is some trick. Come, leave your quiblins, Dorothy.   110
DOL
  Look out, and see.
SUBTLE   Art thou in earnest?
DOL   'Slight,
  Forty o' the neighbours are about him, talking.
FACE
  'Tis he, by this good day.
DOL   'Twill prove ill day,
  For some on us.
FACE   We are undone, and taken.
DOL
  Lost, I am afraid.
SUBTLE   You said he would not come,   115
  While there died one a week, within the liberties.
FACE
  No: 'twas within the walls.
SUBTLE   Was't so? Cry you mercy:
  I thought the liberties. What shall we do now, Face?
FACE
  Be silent: not a word, if he call, or knock.
  I'll into mine old shape again, and meet him,   120
  Of Jeremy, the butler. I' the mean time,
  Do you two pack up all the goods, and purchase,

110 *quiblins* tricks
116 *liberties* the area surrounding a town subject to municipal authority
122 *purchase* gains

[157]

That we can carry i' the two trunks. I'll keep him
Off for today, if I cannot longer: and then
At night, I'll ship you both away to Ratcliff,   125
Where we'll meet tomorrow, and there we'll share.
Let Mammon's brass, and pewter keep the cellar:
We'll have another time for that. But, Dol,
Pray thee, go heat a little water, quickly,
Subtle must shave me. All my Captain's beard   130
Must off, to make me appear smooth Jeremy.
You'll do't?

SUBTLE   Yes, I'll shave you, as well as I can.

FACE

And not cut my throat, but trim me?

SUBTLE   You shall see, sir.

[*Exeunt* SUBTLE, FACE, DOL]

Act V, Scene i

[*In the street outside Lovewit's house*]

[*Enter*] LOVEWIT, NEIGHBOURS

LOVEWIT

Has there been such resort, say you?

NEIGHBOUR 1   Daily, sir.

NEIGHBOUR 2

And nightly, too.

NEIGHBOUR 3   Ay, some as brave as lords.

NEIGHBOUR 4

Ladies, and gentlewomen.

NEIGHBOUR 5   Citizen's wives.

NEIGHBOUR 1

And knights.

NEIGHBOUR 6 In coaches.

NEIGHBOUR 2   Yes, and oyster-women.

---

125 *Ratcliff* a riverside district of east London
126 *there* then Q

  1 *resort* thronging of people
  4 *oyster-women* female oyster sellers

NEIGHBOUR 1
　Beside other gallants.
NEIGHBOUR 3　　　　　Sailors' wives.
NEIGHBOUR 4　　　　　　　　Tobacco-men.　　　　　　　　5
NEIGHBOUR 5
　Another Pimlico!
LOVEWIT　　　　　What should my knave advance,
　To draw this company? He hung out no banners
　Of a strange calf, with five legs, to be seen?
　Or a huge lobster, with six claws?
NEIGHBOUR 6　　　　　　　No, sir.
NEIGHBOUR 3
　We had gone in then, sir.
LOVEWIT　　　　　　He has no gift　　　　　　10
　Of teaching i' the nose, that e'er I knew of!
　You saw no bills set up, that promised cure
　Of agues, or the toothache?
NEIGHBOUR 2　　　　　　No such thing, sir.
LOVEWIT
　Nor heard a drum struck, for baboons, or puppets?
NEIGHBOUR 5
　Neither, sir.
LOVEWIT　　What device should he bring forth now!　　15
　I love a teeming wit, as I love my nourishment.
　Pray God he ha' not kept such open house,
　That he hath sold my hangings, and my bedding:
　I left him nothing else. If he have eat 'em,
　A plague o' the moth, say I. Sure he has got　　　20
　Some bawdy pictures, to call all this ging;
　The Friar, and the Nun; or the new motion
　Of the Knight's courser, covering the Parson's mare;

6　*Pimlico* not the present Pimlico but a place in Hoxton (then Hogsden), east of the city,
　famous for pies and 'Pimlico' nut-brown ale
　advance produce
8　*calf . . . legs* see *Bartholmew Fair*, V.iv.81–3, where this calf has matured to a bull. Such
　deformities were great money-spinners
11　*teaching i' the nose* i.e. with an impressive twang; la di da
14　*drum struck* to 'drum up' a crowd
21　*ging* gang; crowd
22　*motion* puppet show

The boy of six year old, with the great thing:
Or 't may be, he has the fleas that run at tilt, 25
Upon a table, or some dog to dance?
When saw you him?

NEIGHBOUR 1   Who sir, Jeremy?

NEIGHBOUR 2   Jeremy butler?
We saw him not this month.

LOVEWIT   How!

NEIGHBOUR 4   Not these five weeks, sir.

NEIGHBOUR 1
These six weeks, at the least.

LOVEWIT   Y' amaze me, neighbours!

NEIGHBOUR 5
Sure, if your worship know not where he is, 30
He's slipped away.

NEIGHBOUR 6   Pray God, he be not made away!

LOVEWIT
Ha? It's no time to question, then.   *He knocks*

NEIGHBOUR 6   About
Some three weeks since, I heard a doleful cry,
As I sat up, a-mending my wife's stockings.

LOVEWIT
This's strange! That none will answer! Didst thou hear 35
A cry, saist thou?

NEIGHBOUR 6   Yes, sir, like unto a man
That had been strangled an hour, and could not speak.

NEIGHBOUR 2
I heard it too, just this day three weeks, at two o'clock
Next morning.

LOVEWIT   These be miracles, or you make 'em so!
A man an hour strangled, and could not speak, 40
And both you heard him cry?

NEIGHBOUR 3   Yes, downward, sir.

LOVEWIT
Thou art a wise fellow: give me thy hand I pray thee.
What trade art thou on?

---

24 *The boy . . . thing* 'but of all the sights that ever were in London since I married, methinks the little child that was so fair grown about the members was the prettiest' Francis Beaumont, *The Knight of the Burning Pestle*, III.273–5

25 *at tilt* in a duel or tilting match

29 NEIGHBOUR 1 ed. Q, F omit 1

NEIGHBOUR 3   A smith, and't please your worship.

LOVEWIT

A smith? Then, lend me thy help, to get this door open.

NEIGHBOUR 3

That I will presently, sir, but fetch my tools—   45

[*Exit* NEIGHBOUR 3]

NEIGHBOUR 1

Sir, best to knock again, afore you break it.

Act V, Scene ii

LOVEWIT

I will. [*Knocks*]

[FACE, *clean-shaven as Jeremy, opens door*]

FACE   What mean you, sir?

NEIGHBOURS 1, 2, 4   O, here's Jeremy!

FACE

Good sir, come from the door.

LOVEWIT   Why! What's the matter?

FACE

Yet farther, you are too near, yet.

LOVEWIT   I'the name of wonder!

What means the fellow?

FACE   The house, sir, has been visited.

LOVEWIT

What? With the plague? Stand thou then farther.

FACE   No, sir,   5

I had it not.

LOVEWIT   Who had it then? I left

None else, but thee, i'the house!

FACE   Yes, sir. My fellow,

The cat, that kept the buttery, had it on her

A week, before I spied it: but I got he

Conveyed away, i'the night. And so I shut   10

The house up for a month—

---

1 The trick used in this scene resembles the one played by the servant Tranio on his master
Theropides in Plautus' *Mostellaria*

LOVEWIT   How!

FACE   Purposing then, sir,
    T'have burnt rose-vinegar, treacle, and tar,
    And, ha' made it sweet, that you should ne'er ha' known it:
    Because I knew the news would but afflict you, sir.

LOVEWIT
    Breathe less, and farther off. Why, this is stranger!   15
    The neighbours tell me all, here, that the doors
    Have still been open—

FACE   How, sir!

LOVEWIT   Gallants, men, and women,
    And of all sorts, tag-rag, been seen to flock here
    In threaves, these ten weeks, as to a second Hogsden,
    In days of Pimlico, and Eye-bright!

FACE   Sir,   20
    Their wisdoms will not say so!

LOVEWIT   Today, they speak
    Of coaches, and gallants; one in a French hood,
    Went in, they tell me: and another was seen
    In a velvet gown, at the window! Divers more
    Pass in and out!

FACE   They did pass through the doors then,   25
    Or walls, I assure their eyesights, and their spectacles;
    For here, sir, are the keys: and here have been,
    In this my pocket, now, above twenty days!
    And for before, I kept the fort alone, there.
    But, that 'tis yet not deep i'the afternoon,   30
    I should believe my neighbours had seen double
    Through the black pot, and made these apparitions!
    For, on my faith, to your worship, for these three weeks,
    And upwards, the door has not been opened.

LOVEWIT   Strange!

NEIGHBOUR 1
    Good faith, I think I saw a coach!

---

19 *threaves* throngs
   Hogsden Hoxton
20 *Eye-bright* a drinking place which made its name before Pimlico. H.&S. quote '*Pimlico.
   Or Runne Red-Cap: Eye-bright*, (so fam'd of late for *Beere*)/Although thy *Name* be
   numbered heere,/Thine ancient *Honors* now runne low;/Thou art struck blind by
   Pimlyco.' Perhaps its famous beer contained the herb Eyebright (*Euphrasia*)
24 *window* windore Q, F
32 *apparitions* the English title of Plautus' *Mostellaria* is *The Haunted House*

NEIGHBOUR 2   And I too,   35
 I'd ha' been sworn!
LOVEWIT   Do you but think it now?
 And but one coach?
NEIGHBOUR 4   We cannot tell, sir: Jeremy
 Is a very honest fellow.
FACE   Did you see me at all?
NEIGHBOUR 1
 No. That we are sure on.
NEIGHBOUR 2   I'll be sworn o' that.
LOVEWIT
 Fine rogues, to have your testimonies built on!   40

          [*Enter* NEIGHBOUR 3 *with his tools*]

NEIGHBOUR 3
 Is Jeremy come?
NEIGHBOUR 1   O, yes, you may leave your tools,
 We were deceived, he says.
NEIGHBOUR 2   He's had the keys:
 And the door has been shut these three weeks.
NEIGHBOUR 3   Like enough.
LOVEWIT
 Peace, and get hence, you changelings.

          [*Enter* SURLY *and* MAMMON]

FACE   Surly come!
 And Mammon made acquainted? They'll tell all.   45
 (How shall I beat them off? What shall I do?)
 Nothing's more wretched, than a guilty conscience.

Act V, Scene iii

SURLY
 No, sir, he was a great physician. This,

---

42   NEIGHBOUR 1 MEI Q
44   *changelings* those of unstable wits; so-called because they change their stories
47   *Mostellaria* 544: 'Nihil est miserius quam animus hominis conscius'

It was no bawdy-house: but a mere chancel.
You knew the lord, and his sister.
MAMMON   Nay, good Surly—
SURLY
    The happy word, 'be rich'—
MAMMON   Play not the tyrant—
SURLY
    Should be today pronounced, to all your friends.   5
    And where be your andirons now? And your brass pots?
    That should ha' been golden flagons, and great wedges?
MAMMON
    Let me but breathe. What! They ha' shut their doors,
    Me thinks!   MAMMON *and* SURLY *knock*
SURLY   Ay, now, 'tis holiday with them.
MAMMON   Rogues,
    Cozeners, imposters, bawds.
FACE   What mean you, sir?   10
MAMMON
    To enter if we can.
FACE   Another man's house?
    Here is the owner, sir. Turn you to him,
    And speak your business.
MAMMON   Are you, sir, the owner?
LOVEWIT
    Yes, sir.
MAMMON And are those knaves, within, your cheaters?
LOVEWIT
    What knaves? What cheaters?
MAMMON   Subtle, and his Lungs.   15
FACE
    The gentleman is distracted, sir! No lungs,
    Nor lights ha' been seen here these three weeks, sir,
    Within these doors, upon my word!
SURLY   Your word,
    Groom arrogant?
FACE   Yes, sir, I am the housekeeper
    And know the keys ha' not been out o' my hands.   20

2 *chancel* the part of the church used for priestly offices
16 *distracted* out of his wits
16–17 *lungs . . . lights* puns on the anatomical sense of 'lights': entrails

[164]

SURLY
 This's a new Face?

FACE   You do mistake the house, sir!
 What sign was't at?

SURLY   You rascal! This is one
 O' the confederacy. Come, let's get officers,
 And force the door.

LOVEWIT   Pray you stay, gentlemen.

SURLY
 No, sir, we'll come with warrant.

MAMMON   Ay, and then,   25
 We shall ha' your doors open.

          [*Exeunt* SURLY, MAMMON]

LOVEWIT   What means this?

FACE
 I cannot tell, sir!

NEIGHBOUR 1   These are two o' the gallants,
 That we do think we saw.

FACE   Two o' the fools?
 You talk as idly as they. Good faith, sir,
 I think the moon has crazed 'em all!

      [*Enter* KASTRIL]

         (O me,   30
 The angry boy come too? He'll make a noise,
 And ne'er away till he have betrayed us all.)

          KASTRIL *knocks*

KASTRIL
 What rogues, bawds, slaves, you'll open the door anon,
 Punk, cockatrice, my suster. By this light
 I'll fetch the marshal to you. You are a whore,   35
 To keep your castle—

FACE   Who would you speak with, sir?

---

22 *sign* public eating houses, taverns and brothels all had signs like modern pub signs
30 *the moon* creator of lunacy
34 *cockatrice* a serpent, usually identified with the death-glancing Basilisk. Here it is used
  partly for its association with 'cock' (it was often used for prostitutes)

KASTRIL

 The bawdy Doctor, and the cozening Captain,
 And Puss my suster.

LOVEWIT   This is something, sure!

FACE

 Upon my trust, the doors were never open, sir.

KASTRIL

 I have heard all their tricks, told me twice over,   40
 By the fat knight, and the lean gentleman.

LOVEWIT

 Here comes another.

                    [*Enter* ANANIAS, TRIBULATION]

FACE   Ananias too?
 And his pastor?

TRIBULATION   The doors are shut against us.

                              They beat too, at the door

ANANIAS

 Come forth, you seed of sulphur, sons of fire,
 Your stench, it is broke forth: abomination   45
 Is in the house.

KASTRIL   Ay, my suster's there.

ANANIAS   The place,
 It is become a cage of unclean birds.

KASTRIL

 Yes, I will fetch the scavenger, and the constable.

TRIBULATION

 You shall do well.

ANANIAS   We'll join, to weed them out.

KASTRIL

 You will not come then? Punk, device, my suster!   50

---

44   *sulphur, sons of fire* Vipers, Sonnes of Belial Q
45   *stench, it* wickednesse Q
46   *Ay,* not in Q
47   *cage . . . birds* see IV.vii. 53 and *Revelation* xviii.2
48   *Yes* I (i.e. Ay) Q
48   *scavenger* officer responsible for keeping streets clean and orderly
50   *Punk, device* perhaps by analogy with 'point-device' (faultlessly proper in dress). But
     'device' may be an independent noun in his list of insults; in which case he is calling his
     sister a whore and a contraption

ANANIAS

  Call her not sister. She is a harlot, verily.

KASTRIL

  I'll raise the street.

LOVEWIT   Good gentlemen, a word.

ANANIAS

  Satan, avoid, and hinder not our zeal.

           [*Exeunt* ANANIAS, TRIBULATION, KASTRIL]

LOVEWIT

  The world's turned Bedlam.

FACE   These are all broke loose,

  Out of St. Katherine's, where they use to keep,   55

  The better sort of mad folks.

NEIGHBOUR 1   All these persons

  We saw go in, and out, here.

NEIGHBOUR 2   Yes, indeed, sir.

NEIGHBOUR 3

  These were the parties.

FACE   Peace, you drunkards. Sir,

  I wonder at it! Please you, to give me leave

  To touch the door, I'll try, and the lock be changed.   60

LOVEWIT

  It mazes me!

FACE   Good faith, sir, I believe,

  There's no such thing. 'Tis all *deceptio visus*.

  (Would I could get him away.)

                      DAPPER *cries out within*

DAPPER   Master Captain, master Doctor.

LOVEWIT

  Who's that?

FACE   (Our clerk within, that I forgot!) I know not, sir.

---

  53 *avoid* clear off

  55 *St. Katherine's* in fact the Hospital of St. Mary 'that was prouided for poore priests, and others, men and women in the Citty of London, that were fallen into frensie or losse of their memory' (Stow, ii, 143). This had been taken over by the Hospital of St. Katherine (on the north side of the Thames, just east of the Tower)

  60 *and* either 'even if' or 'and see if'

  62 *deceptio visus* an optical illusion

DAPPER
   For God's sake, when will her Grace be at leisure?
FACE   Ha!   65
   Illusions, some spirit o' the air: (his gag is melted,
   And now he sets out the throat.)
DAPPER   I am almost stifled—
FACE
   (Would you were altogether.)
LOVEWIT   'Tis i' the house.
   Ha! List.
FACE   Believe it, sir, i' the air!
LOVEWIT   Peace, you—
DAPPER
   Mine aunt's Grace does not use me well.
SUBTLE [*within*]   You fool,   70
   Peace, you'll mar all.
FACE   Or you will else, you rogue.
LOVEWIT
   O, is it so? Then you converse with spirits!
   Come sir. No more o' your tricks, good Jeremy,
   The truth, the shortest way.
FACE   Dismiss this rabble, sir.
   What shall I do? I am catched.
LOVEWIT   Good neighbours,   75
   I thank you all. You may depart.   [*Exeunt* NEIGHBOURS]
                        Come sir,
   You know that I am an indulgent master:
   And therefore, conceal nothing. What's your med'cine,
   To draw so many several sorts of wild-fowl?
FACE
   Sir, you were wont to affect mirth, and wit: 80
   (But here's no place to talk on't i' the street.)
   Give me but leave, to make the best of my fortune,
   And only pardon me th'abuse of your house:
   It's all I beg. I'll help you to a widow,
   In recompense, that you shall gi' me thanks for,   85
   Will make you seven years younger, and a rich one.
   'Tis but your putting on a Spanish cloak,

   67   *sets out the throat* raises his voice

[168]

I have her within. You need not fear the house,
It was not visited.
LOVEWIT   But by me, who came
Sooner than you expected.
FACE   It is true, sir.   90
'Pray you forgive me.
LOVEWIT   Well: let's see your widow.

> [*Exeunt* LOVEWIT, FACE]

Act V, Scene iv

[*Inside Lovewit's house*]

[*Enter* SUBTLE, DAPPER]

SUBTLE
How! Ha' you eaten your gag?
DAPPER   Yes faith, it crumbled
Away i' my mouth.
SUBTLE   You ha' spoiled all then.
DAPPER   No,
I hope my aunt of Fairy will forgive me.
SUBTLE
Your aunt's a gracious lady: but in troth
You were to blame.
DAPPER   The fume did overcome me,   5
And I did do't to stay my stomach. 'Pray you
So satisfy her Grace. Here comes the Captain.

[*Enter* FACE]

FACE
How now! Is his mouth down?
SUBTLE   Ay! He has spoken!
FACE
(A pox, I heard him, and you too.) He's undone, then.
(I have been fain to say, the house is haunted   10
With spirits, to keep churl back.

---

7 s.d. *Enter* FACE who might now need a false beard since he was shaved at the end of Act
   IV (IV.vii.130–1)
8 *mouth down* gag gone
11 *churl* countryman

SUBTLE   And hast thou done it?
FACE
  Sure, for this night.
SUBTLE   Why, then triumph, and sing
  Of Face so famous, the precious king
  Of present wits.
FACE   Did you not hear the coil,
  About the door?
SUBTLE   Yes, and I dwindled with it.)   15
FACE
  Show him his aunt, and let him be dispatched:
  I'll send her to you.   [*Exit* FACE]
SUBTLE   Well sir, your aunt her Grace,
  Will give you audience presently, on my suit,
  And the Captain's word, that you did not eat your gag,
  In any contempt of her Highness.
DAPPER   Not I, in troth, sir.   20

          [*Enter*] DOL *like the Queen of Fairy*

SUBTLE
  Here she is come. Down o' your knees, and wriggle:
  She has a stately presence. Good. Yet nearer,
  And bid, God save you.
DAPPER   Madam.
SUBTLE   And your aunt.
DAPPER
  And my most gracious aunt, God save your Grace.
DOL
  Nephew, we thought to have been angry with you: 25
  But that sweet face of yours, hath turned the tide,
  And made it flow with joy, that ebbed of love.
  Arise, and touch our velvet gown.
SUBTLE   The skirts,
  And kiss 'em. So.
DOL   Let me now stroke that head,
  Much, nephew, shalt thou win; much shalt thou spend;   30
  Much shalt thou give away: much shalt thou lend.

  14 *coil* row
  23 *you* her Q

[170]

SUBTLE
  (Ay, much, indeed.) Why do you not thank her Grace?
DAPPER
  I cannot speak, for joy.
SUBTLE   See, the kind wretch!
  Your Grace's kinsman right.
DOL   Give me the bird.
  Here is your fly in a purse, about your neck, cousin,   35
  Wear it, and feed it, about this day se'ennight,
  On your right wrist—
SUBTLE   Open a vein, with a pin,
  And let it suck but once a week: till then,
  You must not look on't.
DOL   No. And, kinsman,
  Bear yourself worthy of the blood you come on.   40
SUBTLE
  Her Grace would ha' you eat no more Woolsack pies,
  Nor Dagger frume'ty.
DOL   Nor break his fast,
  In Heaven, and Hell.
SUBTLE   She's with you everywhere!
  Nor play with costermongers, at mum-chance, tray-trip,
  God-make-you-rich, (whenas your aunt has done it:) but keep   45
  The gallantest company, and the best games—
DAPPER   Yes, sir.
SUBTLE
  Gleek and primero: and what you get, be true to us.
DAPPER
  By this hand, I will.
SUBTLE   You may bring's a thousand pound,
  Before tomorrow night, (if but three thousand,

---

33   *kind* showing the affections of kin
34   *bird* Dapper's fly-familiar is a bird in fairyland
36   *se'ennight* week (seven nights)
41   *Woolsack pies* pies from the Woolsack tavern – probably the one outside Aldgate
42   *Dagger frume'ty* see I.i.191
43   *Heaven, and Hell* drinking places in Westminster, popular with lawyers' clerks.
      Hell had once been a debtor's prison
44   *mum-chance, tray-trip* dice games
45   *God-make-you-rich* a kind of backgammon
47   *Gleek and primero* see II.iii.284–5

Be stirring) an' you will.

DAPPER   I swear, I will then.   50

SUBTLE

Your fly will learn you all games.

FACE [*within*]   Ha' you done there?

SUBTLE

Your grace will command him no more duties?

DOL   No:

But come, and see me often. I may chance
To leave him three or four hundred chests of treasure,
And some twelve thousand acres of Fairyland: 55
If he game well, and comely, with good gamesters.

SUBTLE

There's a kind aunt! Kiss her departing part.
But you must sell your forty mark a year, now:

DAPPER

Ay, sir, I mean.

SUBTLE   Or, gi't away: pox on't.

DAPPER

I'll gi't mine aunt. I'll go and fetch the writings.   60

SUBTLE

'Tis well, away.   [*Exit* DAPPER]

                    [*Enter* FACE]

FACE   Where's Subtle?

SUBTLE   Here. What news?

FACE

Drugger is at the door, go take his suit,
And bid him fetch a parson, presently:
Say, he shall marry the widow. Thou shalt spend
A hundred pound by the service!   [*Exit* SUBTLE]
                              Now, queen Dol,   65

51 *learn* teach
50 *an'* if Q
50 *an'you will* should you feel like it
51 *learn* teach
55 *twelve* fiue Q
56 *comely* (adv.) 'comelily'
57 *her departing part* i.e. her backside
58 *your* Q; you F
59 *pox* A pox Q
60 DAPPER FAC. Q, F
64 *spend* have to spend; i.e. gain

    Ha' you packed up all?

DOL   Yes.

FACE   And how do you like

    The lady Pliant?

DOL   A good dull innocent.

             [*Enter* SUBTLE]

SUBTLE

    Here's your Hieronimo's cloak, and hat.

FACE   Give me 'em.

SUBTLE

    And the ruff too?

FACE   Yes, I'll come to you presently.   [*Exit* FACE]

SUBTLE

    Now, he is gone about his project, Dol,   70

    I told you of, for the widow.

DOL   'Tis direct

    Against our articles.

SUBTLE   Well, we'll fit him, wench.

    Hast thou gulled her of her jewels, or her bracelets?

DOL

    No, but I will do't.

SUBTLE   Soon at night, my Dolly,

    When we are shipped, and all our goods aboard,   75

    Eastward for Ratcliff; we will turn our course

    To Brainford, westward, if thou saist the word:

    And take our leaves of this o'erweening rascal,

    This peremptory Face.

DOL   Content, I am weary of him.

SUBTLE

    Th' hast cause, when the slave will run a-wiving, Dol,   80

    Against the instrument, that was drawn between us.

DOL

    I'll pluck his bird as bare as I can.

SUBTLE   Yes, tell her,

    She must by any means, address some present

    To th' cunning man; make him amends, for wronging

---

72 *articles* of faith (their 'venture tripartite', I.i.135)

77 *Brainford* Brentford, in Middlesex

81 *instrument* agreement

His art with her suspicion; send a ring; 85
Or chain of pearl; she will be tortured else
Extremely in her sleep, say: and ha' strange things
Come to her. Wilt thou?
DOL   Yes.
SUBTLE   My fine flitter-mouse,
My bird o'the night; we'll tickle it at the Pigeons,
When we have all, and may unlock the trunks, 90
And say, this's mine, and thine, and thine, and mine—

                                   They kiss

                    [*Enter* FACE]

FACE
What now, a-billing?
SUBTLE   Yes, a little exalted
In the good passage of our stock-affairs.
FACE
Drugger has brought his parson, take him in, Subtle,
And send Nab back again, to wash his face. 95
SUBTLE
I will: and shave himself?
FACE   If you can get him.   [*Exit* SUBTLE]
DOL
You are hot upon it, Face, what e'er it is!
FACE
A trick, that Dol shall spend ten pound a month by.

                  [*Enter* SUBTLE]

Is he gone?
SUBTLE   The chaplain waits you i'the hall, sir.
FACE
I'll go bestow him.   [*Exit* FACE]
DOL   He'll now marry her, instantly. 100

---

88 *flitter-mouse* bat
89 *tickle it* live it up
    the Pigeons the Three Pigeons in Brentford market place (closed in 1916); John Lowin,
    the actor who played Mammon, kept it in the Commonwealth period
92 *a-billing* a pun for the audience who have witnessed Dol and Subtle tot up their gains
95 *Nab* him Q
100 *bestow* conduct

SUBTLE

　He cannot, yet, he is not ready. Dear Dol,
　Cozen her of all thou canst. To deceive him
　Is no deceit, but justice, that would break
　Such an inextricable tie as ours was.

DOL

　Let me alone to fit him.

　　　　　　　　[*Enter* FACE]

FACE　　　　　　　Come, my venturers,　　　　　105
　You ha' packed up all? Where be the trunks? Bring forth.

SUBTLE

　Here.

FACE　Let's see 'em. Where's the money?

SUBTLE　　　　　　　　　　　　Here,
　In this.

FACE　　Mammon's ten pound: eight score before.
　The Brethren's money, this. Drugger's, and Dapper's.
　What paper's that?

DOL　　　　　　The jewel of the waiting maid's,　　110
　That stole it from her lady, to know certain—

FACE

　If she should have precedence of her mistress?

DOL　　　　　　　　　　　　　　　Yes.

FACE

　What box is that?

SUBTLE　　　　　The fish-wives' rings, I think:
　And th' ale-wives' single money. Is't not Dol?

DOL

　Yes: and the whistle, that the sailor's wife　　　　115
　Brought you, to know, and her husband were with Ward.

102–4　*To deceive . . . ours was* the word order is Latinate and confusing. A more usual order
　　　would be 'To deceive him that would break such an inextricable tie as ours was, is no
　　　deceit, but justice'

114　*single money* small change

116　*and* whether
　　　Ward a notorious pirate. Andrew Barker, who had been made captive by him, published
　　　a pamphlet about his captor in 1609. Robert Daborne's play, *A Christian turn'd Turke: or
　　　the Tragicall Lives and Deaths of Two Famous Pyrates, Ward and Dansiker*, was acted in
　　　1609 or 1610

FACE

    We'll wet it tomorrow: and our silver beakers,
    And tavern cups. Where be the French petticoats,
    And girdles, and hangers?

SUBTLE   Here, i' the trunk,
    And the bolts of lawn.

FACE   Is Drugger's damask, there?   120
    And the tobacco?

SUBTLE   Yes.

FACE   Give me the keys.

DOL

    Why you the keys!

SUBTLE   No matter, Dol: because
    We shall not open 'em, before he comes.

FACE

    'Tis true, you shall not open them, indeed:
    Nor have 'em forth. Do you see? Not forth, Dol.

DOL   No!   125

FACE

    No, my smock-rampant. The right is, my master
    Knows all, has pardoned me, and he will keep 'em.
    Doctor, 'tis true (you look) for all your figures:
    I sent for him, indeed. Wherefore, good partners,
    Both he, and she, be satisfied: for, here   130
    Determines the indenture tripartite,
    Twixt Subtle, Dol, and Face. All I can do
    Is to help you over the wall, o' the back-side;
    Or lend you a sheet, to save your velvet gown, Dol.
    Here will be officers, presently; bethink you,   135
    Of some course suddenly to scape the dock:
    For thither you'll come else.   *Some knock*

SUBTLE   Hark you, thunder.
    You are a precious fiend!

---

117 *wet it* i.e. wet our whistles
119 *hangars* loops on sword belts from which swords could be hung
120 *bolts* rolls
128 *for your figures* in spite of all your astrological charts; i.e. you never foresaw this
129 *I sent . . . indeed* not true; Face is trying to 'save face'
131 *Determines* terminates
136 *dock* then a word for a rabbit hutch or cage – so part of 'coney-catching' cant.
      Dickens made the word familiar and the metaphor dead

OFFICERS [*without*]   Open the door.

FACE

  Dol, I am sorry for thee i' faith. But hearst thou?
  It shall go hard, but I will place thee somewhere: 140
  Thou shalt ha' my letter to mistress Amo.

DOL   Hang you—

FACE

  Or madam Cæsarean.

DOL   Pox upon you, rogue,
  Would I had but time to beat thee.

FACE   Subtle,
  Let's know where you set up next; I'll send you
  A customer, now and then, for old acquaintance: 145
  What new course ha' you?

SUBTLE   Rogue, I'll hang myself:
  That I may walk a greater devil, than thou,
  And haunt thee i' the flock-bed, and the buttery.

                    [*Exeunt* SUBTLE, FACE, DOL]

Act V, Scene v

        [*Enter*] LOVEWIT [*in Spanish costume*, PARSON]

LOVEWIT

  What do you mean, my masters?

MAMMON [*without*]   Open your door,
  Cheaters, bawds, conjurers.

OFFICER [*without*]   Or we'll break it open.

LOVEWIT

  What warrant have you?

OFFICER   Warrant enough, sir, doubt not:
  If you'll not open it.

LOVEWIT   Is there an officer, there?

141–2 *mistress Amo . . . madam Cæsarean* invented names for brothel-keepers.
        'Amo' is Latin for 'I love' and 'Cæsarean' implies abortion, and perhaps, since Q has
        'Imperiall', suggests a Dominatrix
142 *Caesarean* Imperiall Q
145 *for* for the sake of

OFFICER
  Yes, two, or three for failing.
LOVEWIT   Have but patience,   5
  And I will open it straight.

                    [*Enter* FACE]

FACE   Sir, ha' you done?
  Is it a marriage? Perfect?
LOVEWIT   Yes, my brain.
FACE
  Off with your ruff, and cloak then, be yourself, sir.
SURLY [*without*]
  Down with the door.
KASTRIL [*without*]   'Slight, ding it open.
LOVEWIT   Hold.
  Hold gentlemen, what means this violence?   10

            [*Enter* MAMMON, SURLY, KASTRIL, ANANIAS,
                    TRIBULATION, OFFICERS]

MAMMON
  Where is this collier?
SURLY   And my Captain Face?
MAMMON
  These day-owls.
SURLY   That are birding in men's purses.
MAMMON
  Madam Suppository.
KASTRIL   Doxy, my suster.
ANANIAS   Locusts
  Of the foul pit.
TRIBULATION   Profane as Bel, and the Dragon.
ANANIAS
  Worse than the grasshoppers, or the lice of Egypt.   15

    5 *for failing* to avoid failing
    9 *ding* batter, push
   11 *collier* see I.i.90
   12 *birding* bird-catching
   13 *Madam Suppository* 'suppository' was a slang term for prostitute; perhaps also a sense
        of 'supposed madam' (like 'apocryphal captain')
        suster Q; sister F
   14 *Bel, and the Dragon* two false idols in *Apocrypha*
   15 *grasshoppers . . . lice* two of the plagues visited upon the Egyptians (*Exodus* vii–xii)

LOVEWIT
　　Good gentlemen, hear me. Are you officers,
　　And cannot stay this violence?
OFFICER　　　　　　　　　　　　Keep the peace.
LOVEWIT
　　Gentlemen, what is the matter? Whom do you seek?
MAMMON
　　The chemical cozener.
SURLY　　　　　　　　　And the Captain Pandar.
KASTRIL
　　The nun my suster.
MAMMON　　　　　　Madam Rabbi.
ANANIAS　　　　　　　　　　Scorpions,　　　　　　　20
　　And caterpillars.
LOVEWIT　　　　　Fewer at once, I pray you.
OFFICER
　　One after another, gentleman, I charge you,
　　By virtue of my staff—
ANANIAS　　　　　　　　They are the vessels
　　Of pride, lust, and the cart.
LOVEWIT　　　　　　　Good zeal, lie still,
　　A little while.
TRIBULATION　Peace, Deacon Ananias　　　　　　　25
LOVEWIT
　　The house is mine here, and the doors are open:
　　If there be any such persons, as you seek for,
　　Use your authority, search on o' God's name.
　　I am but newly come to town, and finding
　　This tumult 'bout my door (to tell you true)　　　30
　　It somewhat mazed me; till my man, here, (fearing
　　My more displeasure) told me he had done
　　Somewhat an insolent part, let out my house
　　(Belike, presuming on my known aversion
　　From any air o' the town, while there was sickness)　　35
　　To a Doctor, and a Captain: who, what they are,
　　Or where they be, he knows not.

17　*stay* prevent
20　*nun* a common irony (cf. *Hamlet*, III.i.121)
　　and the cart deserving of the cart
24　*pride, lust, and the cart* shame, and of dishonour Q
32　*he* ed.; not in Q, F

[179]

They enter

MAMMON   Are they gone?

LOVEWIT

You may go in, and search, sir. Here, I find
The empty walls, worse than I left 'em, smoked,
A few cracked pots, and glasses, and a furnace,   40
The ceiling filled with poesies of the candle:
And **MADAM**, with a dildo, writ o' the walls.
Only, one gentlewoman, I met here,
That is within, that said she was a widow—

KASTRIL

Ay, that's my suster. I'll go thump her. Where is she?   45

LOVEWIT

And should ha' married a Spanish Count, but he,
When he came to't, neglected her so grossly,
That I, a widower, am gone through with her.

SURLY

How! Have I lost her then?

LOVEWIT   Were you the Don, sir?

Good faith, now, she does blame y'extremely, and says   50
You swore, and told her, you had ta'en the pains,
To dye your beard, and umbre o'er your face,
Borrowed a suit, and ruff, all for her love;
And then did nothing. What an oversight,
And want of putting forward, sir, was this!   55
Well fare an old harquebuzier, yet,
Could prime his powder, and give fire, and hit,
All in a twinkling.

MAMMON *comes forth*

MAMMON   The whole nest are fled!

LOVEWIT

What sort of birds were they?

---

41 *poesies of the candle* stains caused by candle smoke
42 **MADAM** the typographical joke is from F
    dildo artificial penis
48 *am gone through with her* have gone through the marriage ceremony (with a suggestion
    of literal going through in consummation)
52 *umbre* darken
56 *harquebuzier* musketeer; armed with a harquebus (a kind of long-barrelled gun used in
    the army. Citizens did weapon-training drill at Mile-End Green and other open spaces.
    Justice Shallow reminisces about them in 2. *Henry IV*, III.ii.272 ff)

MAMMON   A kind of choughs,
  Or thievish daws, sir, that have picked my purse   60
  Of eight score, and ten pounds, within these five weeks,
  Beside my first materials; and my goods,
  That lie i' the cellar: which I am glad they ha' left.
  I may have home yet.
LOVEWIT   Think you so, sir?
MAMMON   Ay.
LOVEWIT
  By order of law, sir, but not otherwise.   65
MAMMON
  Not mine own stuff?
LOVEWIT   Sir, I can take no knowledge,
  That they are yours, but by public means.
  If you can bring certificate, that you were gulled of 'em,
  Or any formal writ, out of a court,
  That you did cozen yourself: I will not hold them.   70
MAMMON
  I'll rather lose 'em.
LOVEWIT   That you shall not, sir,
  By me, in troth. Upon these terms they are yours.
  What should they ha' been, sir, turned into gold all?
MAMMON   No.
  I cannot tell. It may be they should. What then?
LOVEWIT
  What a great loss in hope have you sustained?   75
MAMMON
  Not I, the commonwealth has.
FACE   Ay, he would ha' built
  The city new; and made a ditch about it
  Of silver, should have run with cream from Hogsden:
  That, every Sunday in Moorfields, the younkers,
  And tits, and tomboys should have fed on, *gratis*.   80
MAMMON
  I will go mount a turnip cart, and preach
  The end o' the world, within these two months. Surly,
  What! In a dream?

76 *the commonwealth* Mammon has returned to his grandiloquent fantasies of philanthropy
79 *younkers* youths (especially fashionable ones)
80 *tits, and tomboys* young girls and wild girls
81 *turnip cart* a farm-wagon; the type of moveable platform employed by itinerant preachers

SURLY   Must I needs cheat myself,
    With that same foolish vice of honesty!
    Come let us go, and harken out the rogues.   85
    That Face I'll mark for mine, if e'er I meet him.

FACE
    If I can hear of him, sir, I'll bring you word,
    Unto your lodging: for in troth, they were strangers
    To me, I thought 'em honest, as myself, sir.

                            [*Exeunt* MAMMON, SURLY]

        They [TRIBULATION *and* ANANIAS] *come forth*

TRIBULATION
    'Tis well, the Saints shall not lose all yet. Go,   90
    And get some carts—

LOVEWIT   For what, my zealous friends?

ANANIAS
    To bear away the portion of the righteous,
    Out of this den of thieves.

LOVEWIT   What is that portion?

ANANIAS
    The goods, sometimes the orphan's, that the Brethren,
    Bought with their silver pence.

LOVEWIT   What, those i' the cellar,   95
    The knight Sir Mammon claims?

ANANIAS   I do defy
    The wicked Mammon, so do all the Brethren,
    Thou profane man. I ask thee, with what conscience
    Thou canst advance that idol, against us,
    That have the seal? Were not the shillings numbered,   100
    That made the pounds? Were not the pounds told out,
    Upon the second day of the fourth week,
    In the eighth month, upon the table dormant,
    The year, of the last patience of the Saints,
    Six hundred and ten?

LOVEWIT   Mine earnest vehement botcher,   105
    And Deacon also, I cannot dispute with you,

---

   99 *idol* Nemrod Q
 100 *the seal* Revelation ix.4
 103 *table dormant* permanent side-board
 104 *of the last patience of the Saints* i.e. this is the last millenium before Doomsday
 105 *botcher* see III.ii.113

But, if you get you not away the sooner,
I shall confute you with a cudgel.

ANANIAS   Sir.

TRIBULATION
  Be patient Ananias.

ANANIAS   I am strong,
  And will stand up, well girt, against an host,   110
  That threaten Gad in exile.

LOVEWIT   I shall send you
  To Amsterdam, to your cellar.

ANANIAS   I will pray there,
  Against thy house: may dogs defile thy walls,
  And wasps, and hornets breed beneath thy roof,
  This seat of falsehood, and this cave of cozenage.   115

                          [*Exeunt* ANANIAS, TRIBULATION]

                    DRUGGER *enters*

LOVEWIT
  Another too?

DRUGGER   Not I sir, I am no Brother.

LOVEWIT   *He beats him away*
  Away you Harry Nicholas, do you talk?   [*Exit* DRUGGER]

FACE
  No, this was Abel Drugger. *To the Parson*
                          Good sir, go,
  And satisfy him; tell him, all is done:
  He stayed too long a-washing of his face.   120
  The Doctor, he shall hear of him at Westchester;
  And of the Captain, tell him at Yarmouth: or
  Some good port town else, lying for a wind.   [*Exit* PARSON]
  If you get off the angry child, now, sir—

---

111 *Gad in exile* Genesis xlix.19
116 s.d. at 118 F
117 *Harry Nicholas* Hendrick Niclaes, Anabaptist mystic and leader of 'The Family of Love'.
      He came to England during Edward VI's reign. In 1580 Elizabeth issued a proclamation
      against the sect and their publications
121 *Westchester* Chester
124 *get* can get Q

[*Enter* KASTRIL, DAME PLIANT]

KASTRIL   *To his sister*

Come on, you ewe, you have matched most sweetly, ha' you not?   125
Did not I say, I would never ha' you tupped
But by a dubbed boy, to make you a lady tom?
'Slight, you are a mammet! O, I could touse you, now.
Death, mun' you marry with a pox?

LOVEWIT   You lie, boy;
As sound as you: and I am aforehand with you.

KASTRIL   Anon?   130

LOVEWIT

Come, will you quarrel? I will feize you, sirrah.
Why do you not buckle to your tools?

KASTRIL   God's light!
This is a fine old boy, as e'er I saw!

LOVEWIT

What, do you change your copy, now? Proceed,
Here stands my dove: stoop at her, if you dare.   135

KASTRIL

'Slight I must love him! I cannot choose, i' faith!
And I should be hanged for't. Suster, I protest,
I honour thee, for this match.

LOVEWIT   O, do you so, sir?

KASTRIL

Yes, and thou canst take tobacco, and drink, old boy,
I'll give her five hundred pound more, to her marriage,   140
Than her own state.

LOVEWIT   Fill a pipe-full, Jeremy.

FACE

Yes, but go in, and take it, sir.

LOVEWIT   We will.
I will be ruled by thee in anything, Jeremy.

---

126 *tupped* mated (continues the farmyard talk of 1.125)
127 *dubbed boy* knight
128 *mammet* doll; idiot
     touse tousle; shake
129 *mun'you* must you
130 *sound* pox-free
131 *feize* do for; flog; squeeze
132 *buckle . . . tools* get on your weapons
135 *stoop* a term from falconry, appropriate to Kastril (kestrel)

KASTRIL
    'Slight, thou art not hidebound! Thou art a Jovy boy!
    Come let's in, I pray thee, and take our whiffs.   145
LOVEWIT
    Whiff in with your sister, brother boy.
                       [*Exeunt* KASTRIL, DAME PLIANT)
                            That master
    That had received such happiness by a servant,
    In such a widow, and with so much wealth,
    Were very ungrateful, if he would not be
    A little indulgent to that servant's wit,   150
    And help his fortune, though with some small strain
    Of his own candour. Therefore, gentlemen,
    And kind spectators, if I have outstripped
    An old man's gravity, or strict canon, think
    What a young wife, and a good brain may do: 155
    Stretch age's truth sometimes, and crack it too.
    Speak for thyself, knave.
FACE   So I will, sir. Gentlemen,
    My part a little fell in this last scene,
    Yet 'twas *decorum*. And though I am clean
    Got off, from Subtle, Surly, Mammon, Dol,   160
    Hot Ananias, Dapper, Drugger, all
    With whom I traded; yet I put myself
    On you, that are my country: and this pelf,
    Which I have got, if you do quit me, rests
    To feast you often, and invite new guests.   165

THE END

144 *Jovy boy* jovial fellow
145 *I* not in Q
     whiffs smokes
152 *candour* whiteness of soul
154 *canon* regularity
159 *decorum* the classical principle of consistency and fittingness
163 *my country* my jury (chosen from the neighbourhood)
164 *quit* acquit